HWHW

Other books by Sean McNamara

Renegade Mystic

The Pursuit of Spiritual Freedom Through Consciousness Exploration

SEAN MCNAMARA

SIGNAL

AND

NOISE

ADVANCED
PSYCHIC TRAINING
for Remote Viewing,
Clairvoyance, and ESP

SEAN MCNAMARA

Meditation

X

Telekinesis

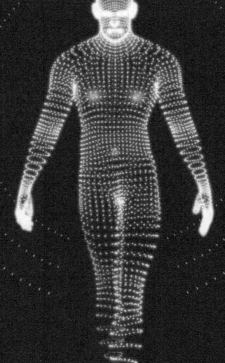

The Mindfulness Practice of Moving Matter
with Subtle Energy and Intention.

by Sean McNamara, author of *Defy Your Limits: The Telekinesis Training Method*

Online Courses at
www.MindPossible.com

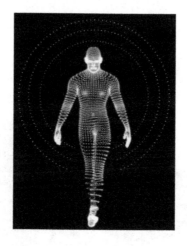

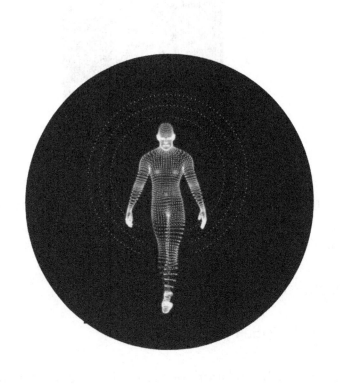

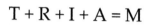

$$T + R + I + A = M$$

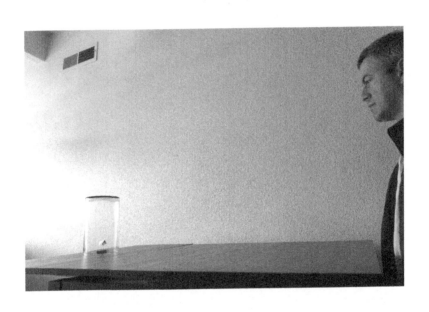

Defy Your Limits

The Telekinesis Training Method

Sean McNamara

Cover Design, Interior and Photography by Sean McNamara

Mind Possible
www.MindPossible.com

First Edition

ISBN 978-0-692-83313-1

1. Metaphysics and Paranormal   2. New Age and Spirituality
3. Self-Help 4. Meditation

For Cierra.

Contents

Acknowledgments

My deepest gratitude goes to my wife, Cierra. She has been a constant source of encouragement and humor from the first day I told her I wanted to learn to move an object from a distance. Her reminders to not believe my own doubts and to not be hard on myself helped me continue what seemed at times, the pursuit of fantasy. Cierra also contributed her energy in editing the book and helping it become what you see now.

I also want to thank my friend Autumn Moran for her constant encouragement. Our regular coffee chats were times for dreaming possibilities, brainstorming, and the first manifestations of ideas.

To my closest meditation students, who I also regard as dear friends, thank you for keeping an open mind when I decided to leave a well-worn path to explore strange trails instead.

Introduction

The resource you are holding in your hands contains specific guidance for learning, practicing, and exploring telekinesis. By understanding and applying these instructions properly you will be able to move a small object enclosed within a glass container. You will do so while seated several feet away from it and without making any physical motion or contact with the object.

It will move through the combined effect of your mental intention and energetic connection, without the assistance of any outside physical influence. This is telekinesis.

I begin this book with the above statement in order to set clear expectations for the reader. It is most likely the case that you are reading this with a sincere interest in telekinesis, also known as psychokinesis or "mind over matter". That is my hope, anyway, because this is how I imagine you while I write this. This is for future generations of aspiring practitioners, and I intend to clear a path for them and for you.

If you follow the path, you will reach the destination. You will reach a place of knowing beyond a doubt that you can move an object across a distance in space. The implications of this ability are profound, and we will discuss them as we go along.

The phrase "to clear a path" implies that the path is initially obscured, or overgrown. Some of our belief systems hide this path by preventing us from even considering new possibilities. There are other obstacles too. Doubt is a troublesome thorn bush, tempting us to turn around and go back to what we already know. Trip hazards such as unreasonable expectations, pride, and stress wait around each bend. Only the most persistent seekers would take the time to separate the weeds from the flowers and keep looking ahead without any outside help.

Another obstacle is the current lack of thoroughly written training material. This is not the case here. I am sharing everything I have learned during my own development. I taught myself to actualize these four levels of telekinesis to the point where I can repeat them with a great deal of consistency.

Rest assured that as your guide, I have personally been where you are going. I have encountered and overcome many of the challenges that you will face. The solutions I share with you will save you much time in your own development.

I won't waste any time by defining telekinesis or giving you a history lesson about it since those are things you can easily learn elsewhere. This is first and foremost, a training manual.

Researchers with advanced degrees in physics, mathematics, and psychology have written books to compile, organize, and report the results of experiments done with practitioners who already know how to actualize the telekinetic effect. Their works are *not* designed to teach someone how to do it.

In contrast, the purpose of *this* book is specifically to do just that, to teach you how to do it. One of my hopes for this text is to teach more people how to do this so that they may be able to work in partnership with those researchers. Together we can help to promote greater social understanding of our natural human potential.

Everything I'm sharing throughout the book has a single purpose, *to shape your mind.* You will not only need to learn the telekinesis techniques; you'll also need to adopt the *attitude* of a practitioner. Like athletes, actors, sales people, and artists, telekinesis practitioners must be committed to training. Intrinsic aspects of training include proper motivation, knowledge, and attitude.

I have been teaching meditation to individuals and groups for over a decade. I have led several retreat programs, and several hundred sessions for local students in my city, Denver, Colorado. I have also met individually with many students to hear their particular questions, challenges, and discoveries.

Because of that, I know firsthand how people successfully work with their own mind. I have also seen how they can become their own worst obstacle. I have seen these same aspects in myself. Based on that past experience, I have included relevant guidance here.

Telekinesis is a specific ability of consciousness and in a way, it is not separate from your whole experience of mind. Therefore, this is about shaping your *whole mind,* and there are important aspects of *the way you think* that need to be attended to during this training.

Compare an Olympic swimmer to a child. The child can learn how to move her arms and legs to execute the breast stroke. What sets the Olympian apart from the child?

She spends many hours each week in the water, refining her stroke. She also sleeps a minimum number of hours each night, and consumes the right quantity and combination of calories each day so that her body grows and recovers enough to become as powerful as possible.

She knows to surround herself with people who support her and believe in her, and to avoid anyone who might impact her psyche in a negative way. She has a coach who keeps her on schedule, who pushes her to do her best, and to cheer her on. Her coach knows what challenges to expect beyond the horizon.

She may also have other mentors and counselors to help her reduce stress and maintain the optimistic, purposeful, and single-focused state of mind that can make the difference between a gold and a silver medal.

The path of developing one's telekinetic ability is just like hers. We'll take a look at what you currently believe is possible, and why you believe it. We'll see what your body-mind connection is like. You will need to make choices regarding which people in your life, if any, you'll share your telekinesis exploration with. We'll also talk about scheduling a training regimen into your daily life and making specific time commitments.

I hope it's becoming clear now that telekinesis isn't just about a method. Your whole *being* is involved, and that implies your sense of self, your sense of *who you are*. A person learning telekinesis is essentially changing their default view of *self*, as well as their view of reality. This is significant. For most of us, change is not only difficult, it invokes a subtle current of conflicting emotions.

You are wading into strange waters, and so it is *the unknown* that may provoke some hesitation. Let me tell you now that telekinesis is safe. There will be no mental or physical straining that could cause injury or illness of any kind, as long as you follow the guidance.

The method is safe because it relies on developing a sense of peace and relaxation within, so as to allow an expansion of subtle energy in the body. So, fear not. Everything I am sharing now is designed to instill one of the most important mental factors you'll need to do this work, *confidence.*

Confidence will give you the energy to read all the material and, so informed, do the practices as prescribed. It will help you hang in there during those practice sessions when it seems like nothing is happening, and it'll prevent you from giving up due to negative mental influences.

The first object of confidence we'll address is for the training method and, by that association, confidence in me. The swimmer and coach in the analogy above have a trusting relationship, and trust has a way of helping a person hear what the other is saying.

I offer you the expectations below to keep in mind while using the training method.

In Level One, you will sit in front of a piece of tin foil delicately balanced on a needle, which we'll call *the object* throughout this book. This object will be fully exposed to the environment, including your body's energy. It may or may not move immediately for you. I know that if you have confidence in the instructions and in the instructor, as well as in yourself, you will persist long enough to move the object through the mobilization of your intention.

You might become able to influence the object at Level One the first time you try, or within a week if you work on it every day for twenty to thirty minutes at a time.

At Level Two, the object will be enclosed in a glass container, thus blocking it from the effect of air movement in the room. Glass is an insulator, and as such it also impedes any electrical effect, such as static. Your hands will gently rest against the sides of the container. If you are unable to move the object after a few attempts, it is your confidence and inspiration which will maintain your commitment to continue your training sessions until it does.

You can expect to work at Level Two between one and four weeks.

When success comes, doubt may arise. If you are like me, the doubt will come from the seemingly rational notion that your hands have heated the glass sufficiently to stimulate convection inside the container. This means that an increase in temperature of the glass contacting your hands has started a cycle of warming and cooling air inside, thus moving it with sufficient force to push the object.

To dispel this doubt, we move to Level Three, in which your hands no longer touch the glass. They will be distant enough from it to remove the possibility of heating it and creating air currents. More importantly, this will remove the previous doubt from your mind.

Level Three will command far more persistence than Level Two for most readers. Again, it will be up to your confidence and inspiration to keep training until you reach success. Level Three can take between one and three months. This will vary depending on how often and how long you train.

Level Four offers the kind of fulfillment that many of us were looking for when we first heard the word "telekinesis". Maybe we didn't know that specific word when we first saw the exaggerated idea of it in movies like Star Wars, E.T., and Harry Potter. My first exposure to the concept came through the 1940 animated movie Fantasia, starring Mickey Mouse as the Sorcerer's Apprentice. In it, he magically takes command over an army of mops. I remember watching them magically dance and spin by Mickey's intention and will.

Imagine yourself now, sitting at a long table. It is several weeks or months since you first read the page you're looking at right now. You have remained steady in your training ever since then. At the far end of the table, at least three or four feet away, sits same object you moved in Levels One, Two, and Three.

There it rests, carefully balanced on the needle. The glass container protects it from the tiniest breeze. Its distance from you removes the possibility of temperature, static, or anything else causing the movement. No part of your body is touching the table. Your hands are of no use here, so they rest idly in your lap.

Imagine what great doubt might arise as you look across the empty space over the table's length, expecting the movement you created in Levels One, Two, and Three, and seeing none.

Was I fooling myself?

Fortunately, your progress through the first three levels will have shown you that the instructions do work when you follow them well enough, as long as you dedicate the necessary amount of time to practice. At that future point, it'll be your prior progress and acquired self-knowledge which will fuel your confidence and passion to go all the way.

All you have to do it *not give up*.

At this stage, doubt is no longer an obstacle and the path is clear. So, you sit patiently, applying the instructions. It's now less about doing something than about doing nothing. There's nothing to apply. You just look on with intention*. Everything else that needs to occur will happen effortlessly because of your training over previous weeks and months.

Here comes the final moment. Your mind is brought into the proper state, your body is relaxed, your intention is steady and fixed. Energy imperceptibly flows across the quiet room. Unexpectedly, you perceive a fresh glint of light shining off a wrinkle in the foil. But you're not quite sure. One millisecond

---

* You will learn how to look and how to use mental intention in more detail soon.

later, you notice new shadows spreading across its surface. Your inner dialogue erupts.

Is it shifting? What's happening?

Quiet! Keep steady! Wait…

Just a few more moments before you lose your internal balance and lose it all.

It begins to turn.

1. Meet Your Coach

There are things I must share with you from the outset because they will help you understand why this book is structured the way that it is, and why I decided to write it in the first place. You'll be better able to understand the training method from my perspective.

I am passionate about teaching. As a young adult, I became interested in meditation and joined a local Buddhist community. This group structured itself so that those interested could be trained to mentor the novice meditators. I had received so much benefit from my own instructor that it was out of a sense of gratitude and natural interest that I became a meditation instructor. Mentoring evolved to periodically leading small classes.

Over time, and in various settings, I continued my development not only as an instructor, but as a teacher, eventually leading retreats ranging from a day to two weeks in length. I viewed this activity as part of my own spiritual development. At the same time, I was (and still am) a regular person with a regular job.

I graduated with a Bachelor's degree in Computer Science and worked in the telecommunications industry for 6 years before needing heart surgery at age twenty-five. It was minor, but the event was enough of a stimulus for me to re-evaluate how I wanted to spend the rest of my life.

After recovering, I went on vacation in Peru, hiking the Inca Trail to Machu Picchu and exploring the natural and historical places of the area. The daily hiking helped me appreciate the gift of having a human body that can move, feel, and receive.

Meeting new people and gaining new experiences every day brought a sense of discovery that had been missing at home, especially while at my cubicle. My recent heart surgery left me counting how many years I might have left in this life, and contemplating how many of them I might spend in that cubicle if I didn't change something soon. This fresh perspective prompted an ultimate decision to quit my job and seek more meaningful work.

In the decades since, I've worked with developmentally disable adults, as a car salesman, as a massage therapist. Today, I'm a real estate agent. The common thread of these jobs is their spirit of service and personal connection.

Extending that spirit into my meditation teaching, I gradually fostered a local meditation group which went from meeting twice a month to twice per week.

One day, while perusing the International Association of Near Death Studies (IANDS) video channel I watched a presentation by Cherylee Black. Cherylee is a Near Death Experiencer who also has telekinetic abilities. In this presentation I watched her turn a shaped piece of tinfoil on a needle which was enclosed in a jar. It stirred something inside of me.

The timing was perfect for me to find this video. It was during a period when many in the meditation group were struggling to maintain a steady practice. I wanted to find a new way to inspire them. I thought that if I could do something special to show them how powerful their own minds were, and that they truly did have an influence on their external world, that it would be of immense help.

I decided to teach myself telekinesis the way I saw Cherylee Black do it. It appeared far more legitimate to me than other examples I'd found online. I already knew the rigor of mind training, so it didn't seem too unreasonable to test myself by applying everything I knew to see if I could do it.

Interconnectedness is a common theme in Buddhism and other spiritual or religious traditions. If I could exhibit telekinesis to my students, I hoped it would illustrate our non-physical connection with our world, and with each other.

Karma, simply defined as "cause and effect" is a notion tightly related to interconnectedness. Why can things or people affect others? Because they are inherently connected. They are in relationship to each other. If they weren't, then the actions of one wouldn't do anything to the other.

Could telekinesis show that our minds and bodies, being subtly connected to the world, are profoundly sensitive to our thoughts, words, and deeds, and to those of others? Could this understanding then bolster my students' interest and resolve to develop their own minds through meditation?

Would it inspire them to practice more regularly and develop themselves further?

The meditation tradition that I had been primarily trained in came with ancient proscriptions against showing any special abilities that might occur as a natural side-effect of spiritual development. Exhibiting any special abilities was traditionally viewed as a prideful activity, a waste of energy, and a cul-de-sac along the path to true spiritual advancement.

Fortunately, I didn't let that hold me back. Just as happens in classrooms, corporations, churches and temples everywhere, one of the communities I was involved with had been spoiled though psychological manipulation, abuse of power, narcissism, etc. by some of the leadership there.

I left that situation, and began to review and challenge many of the spiritual and traditional assumptions I had picked up over the years. For example, I found it suspicious that it was acceptable to venerate authority figures for their special abilities, if they had any, yet if a common person exhibited any then he or she would be looked down upon as egotistical.

This phase of my life included periods of grief, confusion, and resentment. But I emerged renewed, and inspired. It was more important than ever for me to teach in a way that truly empowered the students without promoting an artificial need for dependency from them. I didn't want to recreate the harmful group dynamics of my former community. I was also willing to try something new.

So, one day I placed a piece of folded tinfoil on a needle embedded in an eraser, which served as the base. I covered

Meet Your Coach

the setup with a plain glass vase to protect it from any wind in the room. I had seen videos of people doing it without a glass cover, but I already had doubts about those types of experiments. I inadvertently decided on a much more difficult way to begin. The level of difficulty naturally matched what would be my greatest obstacle: self-doubt.

I tried moving the object for weeks, sometimes it was tin foil, sometimes paper, to no effect. I would sit in front of it anywhere from twenty minutes to nearly an hour at a time, at least five days a week. My wife Cierra, also a meditation teacher, is wonderfully open minded and deeply engaged in her own spiritual path. She knew what I was up to and offered only support and encouragement.

My daily reports to her of disappointment, unmet (and unfair) expectations of myself, and impatience revealed some of the psychological factors that would accompany me even until today. Her patience, encouragement, and sense of humor helped me to not give up and throw everything into a waste basket.

These first weeks were a time of broad experimentation. I felt like a sailor lost at sea without a compass or sextant. I would go in one direction for a period of time, then with no land in sight, choose another and try again, never knowing if I was closer or further away from my destination.

I experimented with the meditative techniques I already knew. They involved specific breathing styles, energy movement, and mental quiescence. I also found what I considered legitimate telekinesis practitioners who had posted helpful tips online. I have immense gratitude for them today. Their guidance proved to be worthwhile.

I eventually succeeded with what I refer to in this book as Level Two, using a glass cover, hands touching the sides. Ever pursued by my own doubts, I worked to prove to myself that it wasn't just my hands heating the glass and moving the air inside. This became Level Three, hands nearby, but not touching it. I reached Level Four about one year after Level One. I was excited to introduce this to my meditation students.

The response was disappointing, however. Most of them simply weren't interested, or were too polite to tell me that they thought it wasn't real.

The mistake was mine. I quickly realized that this was the wrong audience. These meditators wanted to lessen their stress levels, understand their internal psychological experience better, and progress on their own spiritual path. They *already* had the techniques to do those things, so telekinesis was an unnecessary add-on.

I still wanted to share what I had learned though, and I knew where I could find the right audience – on the internet. I began making videos, sharing what I had discovered and encouraging others to try. There were other telekinesis practitioners online who had superior telekinetic abilities. What I had to offer was the ability to communicate clearly with others and to share ideas about consciousness in a helpful way.

Meet Your Coach

Teaching via the internet introduced me to new challenges, though.

Most internet viewers prefer short videos, ideally under two minutes. Intelligently describing, then demonstrating a telekinesis experiment under two minutes is nearly impossible. Fortunately, this book doesn't have that limitation.

People sometimes confuse the ease of watching something being done with the level of effort it takes to do it. Telekinesis, especially at Level One, can appear facile. Yet if some people are unable to succeed right away, they might give up too soon. Since you know that this book is a training system, you understand that this will take work and commitment. I have no doubt that you can do everything I can do, and that it'll probably happen even faster for you because you now have this training method.

When new practitioners email me saying that they've succeeded, it lights up my heart. I know the wonderful feeling of excitement and discovery that they're experiencing, and I share in their joy. I look forward to your success as well.

2. Motivation and Psychology in Telekinesis

Motivation is everything. The word *motivation* means "to stimulate toward action." Without a sense of motivation in mind, we go nowhere, accomplish nothing. At best, we maintain habitual routines and avoid the extra effort needed to try new things and take chances.

Why do you want to learn telekinesis? If you don't have a clear answer, or can't find the right wording for it, perhaps some of the sample motivations below will help you look within and find those words.

I want to be able to do something spectacular, something that few others can do.

I believe in mind over matter, and want to turn that belief into actual experience. I want to see it with my own eyes.

Ever since I was little, I wanted to be a Jedi.

Normal meditation techniques are too boring for me. I want to find a more provocative way to be with my body and mind.

I disagree with materialistic science, and I think that consciousness is something different than the physical brain. Moving an object from a distance is a possible way to illustrate that consciousness extends beyond physical boundaries.

If I can do this, then I know I can do anything I put my mind to.

In my own practice and study of Chi Kung, the movement of chi is a key principle. Since chi is everywhere, I'd like to explore that principle through telekinesis experiments.

I'm an energy healer. I'd like to see if I can use my intention on things outside of the human bio-system. Can I affect something outside the body? Can I see that influence with my own eyes?

I'm aware of concepts like those shared in the movies "The Secret," "What the Bleep Do We Know," and in books like "The Law of Attraction."* However, I want an observable method to really show me the power of intention. If I can move a physical object with my mind, then I'll be confident that I can change other aspects of my life by using my mind, particularly my intention, more effectively.

I have other psi abilities, and want to learn firsthand how telekinesis relates to them, and how it can improve my personal development in other areas.

I believe that we are all sacred beings, integral aspects of the conscious universe and as such, we can all experience these abilities to one degree or another. They are not something granted to you by an external authority. Experiencing this will remind me of my own spiritual sovereignty.

---

* See References

I keep hearing that the human race is at the next stage of evolution, and that more and more people are showing these types of abilities. Maybe it's just because technology allows us to exchange new ideas and methods faster than ever before, and what used to be rare knowledge is becoming well known. Whatever it is, I want to be part of our next stage in the evolution of consciousness.

Do any of the above statements resonate with you? You might not have a solid sense of purpose for doing this yet. As you go along, your purpose should become clearer, and *it needs to*. Without a well-developed motivation, chances are higher that you'll give up without immediate results. If you already know why you're doing this and why it's important to you, then you're off to an excellent start.

Even though you're interested in doing this training, parts of your psyche might be in conflict. Think back to when you first considered getting this book. One part of you may have been excited, and another may have been filled with doubt. The emotional blend of hope, doubt, fear, inspiration and courage is normal for anyone beginning something new and strange. You, as a whole person, are about to *change*.

I recommend making room for all your conflicting thoughts and emotions. Even today, my *inner non-believer** watches everything I do with my telekinesis research. Its favorite tool is doubt. It doubts that any of this is real, and that what I'm doing is worthwhile.

Luckily, I was able to express these doubts to my wife. Doing so brought my *inner non-believer* out of the shadows and into

---

* We'll learn more about our inner non-believer later.

Motivation and Psychology in Telekinesis

the light. I could acknowledge it when it appeared. With my wife's help I could even laugh at its persistence, even as I proved it wrong over and over again.

I can even extend some gratitude to my inner non-believer because it drove me to keep working harder, growing from Level Two to Level Three, then Level Four and beyond to further understand this phenomenon.

My inner non-believer still remains a helpful companion. It seems that I can't eradicate it. Since I'd rather be stuck with a friend than a foe, I've made room for it in my mind, and its presence helps me test my limits.

There are generally *four attitudes** we carry within ourselves. To put it more accurately, these are four default responses that we exhibit when approached by anything that challenges our accepted beliefs about reality.

The *non-believer* I described above is one of them. The other three are the *skeptic*, the *pseudo-skeptic*, and the *believer*. It's important for you to learn about them because it's quite possible that all four will manifest out loud during your training.

They will either help or hinder your progress. This is not only the case with telekinesis, but with any kind of risk-taking that challenges dominant social beliefs about reality and human potential.

---

* When writing this, I drew on definitions from *The End of Materialism, How Evidence of the Paranormal is Bringing Science and Sprit Together*, by Charles T. Tart, Ph.D. His explanation of *scientism* is valuable for anyone interested in psi.

The word "skepticism" is overwhelmingly used for a particular one of its various definitions[*]: "an attitude of doubt or a disposition to incredulity." The dominant use of this definition has spread into the media and everyday use by the public.

Unfortunately, then, when most people refer to themselves as a skeptic, they believe their own *opinion*, which they passively adopted through social conditioning. They take it to be correct even without considering the newest data or doing any research themselves.

I prefer its other definition, "the method of suspended judgment," which is better understood in scientific circles. A true skeptic is a person who is *open minded*, who will not take an idea on faith, but instead reviews the available data and forms a decision based on that. If new data becomes available which contradicts the old, the skeptic is willing to change his or her opinion based on that new information.

I think of the skeptic as a cool-headed personality, slow to come to decisions and comfortable with uncertainty. The skeptic is in no hurry to come to conclusions because he or she has no personal agenda for the results to prove or disprove a theory. Of the *four attitudes*, the true skeptic is the minority. It's constantly challenged by the believer, the non-believer, and the pseudo-skeptic (which is also a type of believer).

The *non-believer* is unwilling and uninterested in considering any data that might support a change in the status quo. When I started finding telekinesis videos online, the non-believer

---

[*] https://www.merriam-webster.com/dictionary/skepticism

was there in the back of my mind making remarks like, "Seriously? Are you kidding me? Why are you even watching this stuff? It's not real!"

When I set up my training area, it made me feel embarrassed with myself for even doing that. It made me paranoid that someone might find out that I was trying this stuff, and that they might think I was lost in a fantasy. Every time I had a success, my inner non-believer suggested an alternative explanation, a reason why it couldn't have possibly been my own intention.

The *believer* is like a well-intentioned friend who has faith in you but has to make up stories to back you up. It's emotional. My believer was there inside me the first time I watched Luke Skywalker pull his X-Wing fighter out of the swamp with Master Yoda's instruction, "Do or do not, there is no try."* As the chill ran up my spine, I just wanted to *believe* so badly that this kind of thing could be true.

You may really believe that telekinesis is real, but there's one problem. You've never *experienced* it yourself, and you have no other data to show that it's real.

The helpful part about the believer is that it's the reason why you considered this book in the first place. It's the reason you began your search at all. It's the aspect of you that will continue the training even when the non-believer and the pseudo-skeptic are telling you to give up because you're just fooling yourself. When a moment of doubt arises, the believer will keep you going.

---

* Star Wars: Episode V – The Empire Strikes Back (1980). Irvin Kershner

When your inner believer and non-believer argue, neither truly wins because neither has a basis of proof. It's simply a battle of emotions. For the skeptic, there is no argument. There is only data, or no data.

So, when your inner believer is urging you on with your exploration, daring you to try new things, listen wholeheartedly. Let it fuel your passion.

Once you have data, otherwise known as *direct experience*, you can share it with others if you choose. But do so as a skeptic, not as a believer. Let people make their own conclusions. People who don't want to change their minds about how the world works, won't, even when given new information. This brings us to the last of the four personalities, the pseudo-skeptic.

The *pseudo-skeptic* is boisterous and a time-waster. It claims to be a true skeptic, and that its arguments are based on science. For example, it'll say things like "Science still hasn't proven that ESP is real." Yet the fact is that many published studies over the last several decades do show that people are able to gain information without the use of the five senses. These studies involve double-blind experiments and multiple subjects. A statistical analysis of the results indicates a psi* effect far beyond chance, or beyond what most folks call "luck."

The pseudo-skeptic either is not aware of these studies because it would rather not look, or it's hoping that you're not aware of them yourself and you take its word for it instead. If

---

* Psychic ability.

a pseudo-skeptic encounters data which gives evidence for psi, it will argue that the experiment was flawed in some way, that the results were skewed, or that the researcher is manipulating the data. Then it will discard the results and continue promoting its preferred beliefs.

Alternately, if the pseudo-skeptic encounters data that contradicts the possibility of psi, it will defend the study vigorously and refuse to consider any conflicting evidence from other studies. This is not science. This is what Charles Tart PhD labeled "scientism" in his book *The End of Materialism*.

Educating yourself about what studies have actually revealed will help counter your inner pseudo-skeptic. Information is power, it gives you a sense of conviction. When you learn what others have discovered, you can use those facts to put the pseudo-skeptic to rest. This is also important when *people* challenge you.

The best data is your own personal experience. At the same time, I strongly recommend that you read these three books: *The End of Materialism* by Charles Tart, PhD; *Supernormal* by Dean Radin, PhD; and *The Reality of ESP: A Physicist's Proof of Psychic Abilities* by Russell Targ, PhD.

These researchers are on the cutting edge of psi research using valid scientific methodology and statistical analysis. They will help you get caught up on what real scientists have learned. You will see that the data show strong evidence for telekinesis and other phenomena. This should give you much encouragement.

Now that you know how to identify your four inner personalities, you can put these characters to good use.

Assign your inner believer the task of cheering you on to discovery. Let the inner non-believer suggest where you can improve your skill or tighten up an experiment to reduce doubt. The inner skeptic will keep track of what works and what doesn't work based on the results, helping you *learn*. Your inner pseudo-skeptic will challenge you to educate yourself.

The best attitude to take *during a training session* is that of a skeptic. When you act and *feel* like a true skeptic, you remain emotionally neutral during the session. This helps you stay relaxed, which you'll learn is vital to success in telekinesis.

If, on the other hand, you train like a believer, the emotions of excitement and hope will devolve into impatience, worry, struggle, and defeat. This will only cause stress, which substantially weakens your potential.

Let your inner believer fully celebrate *after* you succeed at moving the object. Celebration is valuable, at the appropriate time.

Motivation and Psychology in Telekinesis

3. Training Supplies and Recommendations

For Level One

- A long sewing needle or pin.

- A base to insert the upright needle into. You could use a pencil eraser, a cork, a small bar of soap, or a candle. It should not be any kind of material that could carry a static electrical charge. Stick the needle or pin into the base so that the sharpest tip is *up*. This is where the object will be placed. The reason for putting the sharpest tip up is to minimize friction between the object and the needle tip as much as possible.

- A rectangular piece of tinfoil the length of a finger, and about half as wide. Fold the tinfoil lengthwise so that it is shaped like a tent. Then balance the tinfoil upon the needle. Be careful not to pierce or indent the tin foil in the least. Placing it as gently as possible on the needle should prevent it from getting stuck. The piece of tin foil is now your "object."

You could use a similarly sized piece of paper instead, but it may prove more difficult than the tin foil. I weighed both types of objects on an electronic scale and was surprised to see how much heavier paper is than tin foil. Both are extremely lightweight objects, yet the *relative difference* is significant. I recommend starting as light as possible, with tinfoil. After becoming successful through Level Four, you could repeat the exercises with paper.

- A painter's mask, handkerchief, or something else that you can use to cover your nose and mouth to prevent your breath from interfering with the object.

Find a table and chair in a room where there is as little air movement as possible. Close any windows and turn off any devices like fans, air conditioners, or heaters. The air needs to be as still as possible. The table should be cleared of any other objects, especially electronic devices or anything else that could raise doubt about what's causing the object's movement.

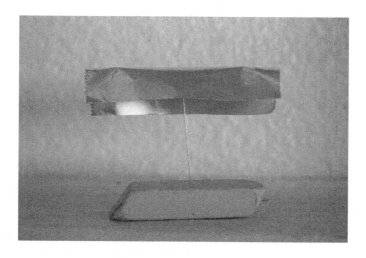

Training Supplies and Recommendations

For Levels Two, Three, and Four

- A glass container with a straight, even lip. You won't need to cover your nose and mouth anymore or close windows because at these levels, the object will be encased in the glass container. I recommend a clear, cylindrical flower vase. The glass should be fairly thin, not thick like a mixing bowl. These types of vases are available in hobby stores, flower shops, and thrift stores.

Be sure that there is no static charge on the glass whatsoever. You can test this by seeing if hair, small pieces of Styrofoam or paper cling to it. If these materials cling to the glass, you'll need to remove the static. The easiest way is to rub a dryer sheet over the interior and exterior surface of the glass.

The reason we want to remove any static charge isn't because it might make the object move, but because *it will prevent it from moving*. Think of it like the needle of a compass, always pointing to the northern pole of the earth's electromagnetic field. We don't want your object to be fixed in one position because of nearby static.

Most glass containers are well designed and will prevent air from passing between the edge and the surface of the table. If you want to be sure that external air movement won't affect the object, you can use masking tape to seal the edge of the container to the table after you've placed it over the object.

When you lower the glass container over the object, do it slowly. The air disturbance will cause the object to spin somewhat, and if it moves too quickly it will fall off the needle. Also, when finally landing the glass onto the table surface, do it gently to prevent a hard impact, causing the object to fall off the needle.

At all levels, the object and the glass container should stay out of direct sunlight or other ambient sources of heat. You should even avoid placing your hot mug of coffee or tea anywhere nearby. Even though these are unlikely to heat the air inside the container, we need to avoid any alternative causes of movement. We're eliminating *doubt* step by step.

Your clothing

You probably know which of your shirts or sweaters accumulate static easily. Don't wear them during telekinesis training. Avoid wearing any clothing that might hold a static charge. Until you're successful, try to wear short sleeved shirts to be sure that your clothes aren't affecting the object. Again, we want to eliminate any alternative causes for the object's movement, or non-movement in the case of static.

Training Supplies and Recommendations

After you've proven to yourself that the object is moving due to your mental and energetic influence, you can continue your training sessions with any clothing you'd like to wear, and with that hot cup of java nearby. By then, you'll be certain that these things are not causing the object's movements.

Your appetite

It's best not to be distracted by hunger, thirst, or other bodily needs during a session. Have a snack and go to the bathroom before you begin. That way, you'll be able to sit in front of the object for a sufficient period of time without needing to get up for any reason. Fighting an urge during the session can weaken your will and attention.

Sleepiness

Sleepiness is a sign that your energy is depleted. You should be well rested before beginning a telekinesis session. Otherwise, you will be easily distracted or discouraged, and give up too soon.

Playing videos or music during a training session

Keep your training room silent and free of distraction. You might think that playing comforting or inspirational music during training might be helpful. However, your intention will be directed toward *perceiving that sound* and listening. Your intentional energy will be divided between two interests, the music and the object.

Your attention will also be directed toward the meaning of the lyrics, how it makes you feel, etc. At that point your energy will go into your mental experience of that song instead of toward the object. The same applies for video. You can't watch a video and successfully do this training at the same time, at least in the very beginning.

We want as much intention to be directed toward the object as possible.

Training Supplies and Recommendations

4. Assumptions Which Impede Success

There is one tremendous obstacle that a person can experience during his or her training. It's not a problem with the instructions, the person's capacity, or with telekinesis itself. The problem comes from inside the person's mind. It is simply an assumption that the person may have picked up at one point in their life.

Nowhere in the training method are practitioners instructed to focus on any parts of the body, not even the hands or forehead. You will engage the position of your hands for Levels One, Two, and Three to one degree or another, but it is the *position of the hands*, and not the hands themselves, which matters.

I've heard from so many new practitioners who struggled because they made the assumption that they were supposed to do something more with their hands. They thought that they should be pushing energy out of their hands, or feeling energy streaming from them.

Beginners often refer to the spiritual/metaphysical concept of chakras, the nexuses of energy transmission in the body's subtle energy. They then wonder, "Why aren't my hand chakras working?" or "How do I activate my hand chakras?"

The roadblock is revealed in their next comment. "I've been focusing on my hands and the object still won't move! It doesn't work!" Or, "When I focus on my hands I feel energy, but I can't make the object move."

They disable themselves by applying their attention and intention *to their hands instead of to the object.*

In the following chapters, you will notice that the instruction is always to keep your eyes and your mind on the object, and not on your hands, your third eye, your heart chakra, or anything else like that. You will learn the principle that *energy follows attention.* If you focus on your hands, the energy will go to your hands instead of to the object.

Similarly, if you focus on your third eye, the energy will go to your head. This is the likely explanation for why some beginners experience headaches or wooziness during their training. They are accidentally flooding their heads with excess energy.

When people makes this mistake, and produce peculiar sensations in their hands, head, or other areas, the experience bolsters this unfortunate assumption. It's understandable because it's a real feeling, something they can easily discern. But it can be a dead end. Instead of the energy going *out there* where it's wanted, it stays in the body instead.

The idea of the third eye, or the brow chakra, is especially problematic. This term is commonly found in online discussion forums, video comment sections, and many

---

* Attention and intention will be discussed in greater detail later.

Assumptions Which Impede Success

spiritual and metaphysical books. Yet the *third eye* means different things to different people in various traditions. Is it a location between the eyebrows? Or is it a few inches above that? Or does it represent the pineal gland in the brain? Or is it something in between, or completely different?

I am not denying the existence or phenomenology of the third eye. What I'm pointing out is that it's a concept found in many different traditions, each with unique modes of training, instruction, and theory. The concept is also misused and misunderstood by people who make up their own ideas about it and spread it over the internet.

Because of this, many new practitioners assume that they need to "open" their third eye in order to do this work. Then they seek advice about how to open it from possibly ill-informed people. Some become disappointed, frustrated, and eventually give up.

I will be clear. You do *not* need to open your third eye to do telekinesis. You do *not* need to push energy out of your hands*. Don't pay any more attention to your hands beyond what's needed to put them in place near the object. At Level Four, the hands won't even be involved in any way at all.

Your subconscious mind has far more knowledge and skill than the conscious mind does. Let *it* do the work of

---

* Having said that, I will remind the reader that this is book only presents one point of view, and that there are many ways to do telekinesis. I have received correspondence from people who say they have indeed used their hands for producing "chi balls" to actualize telekinesis. It's a good reminder of why none of this should become dogma. There's always more than one path to your destination.

stimulating and coordinating your energy. All you have to do is tell it where you want to go, and it'll take you there.

When you drive a car, do you need to know exactly how the internal combustion system works? Do you need to get out and turn the axel with your own hands? Of course, you don't. Your job is to keep your eyes on the road and *look* where you want to go.

The car is useless without the driver, so *be the driver*, not the mechanic. Without intending your destination, you'd just remain parked, in neutral, and you'd wonder why your engine isn't moving the car. Please remember this as you begin your training.

It's likely that you will feel spontaneous energetic sensations throughout your body, including your head and hands. Over time, you'll notice that these sensations come and go without consequence.

Sometimes, when moving the object during a telekinesis session, your hands will feel a little tingly. At other times, in fact *most* of the time in my own experience, you won't feel anything at all.

And still the object moves, without any peculiar body sensations occurring. You don't even need to know how to negotiate the glass barrier. Your subconscious mind, in concert with the surrounding environment, figures that out for you. You just need to *give it time* to figure it out, and that's time spent in each training session.

Assumptions Which Impede Success

In every session, you will reach a particular state of relaxation. Relaxation increases your ability to feel. You will periodically notice movements, temperature shifts, and energetic events in your body. These feelings occur all the time on a daily basis, it's just that we normally don't notice them because we're focused on other things.

Meditation practitioners know this experience well. During a well-settled meditation period, they can feel their heart rate, the peristalsis of their stomach and intestines, and the flow or blockage of energy in the body.

As you read the training instructions below, notice what they advise as well as what they *don't* recommend. Avoid adding outside instructions. With this method, your attention is directed to the object, nowhere else.

5. Level One*

The Level One instructions will be brief and simple compared to Level Two. This is because you will likely find success with Level One with relative ease, before you even have the opportunity to apply all the instructions given later on in the book. If you remain unsuccessful after many attempts at Level One, read the instructions for Level Two and apply them here.**

You will want to read through the Level One instructions completely before beginning your session to get an overall picture of the technique.

Set up your training area per the instructions in the chapter *Training Supplies and Recommendations.* Have a seat, with the object before you on the table. As you adjust your seating position, the air disturbance will move the object, so try to move slowly.

---

* Estimated time for success: less than one week
** The reader might benefit from reading the entire book before beginning any of the actual training so as to be informed as much as possible.

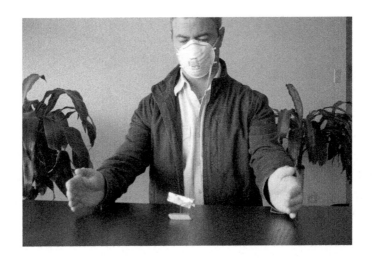

Arms and Hands

Begin by slowly positioning your arms widely, with your hands at the height of the object, hovering over the surface of the table. Your palms should be facing the object.

Eyes

Look at the surface of the object, and nothing else. Remember that energy follows attention. For this training, *where your eyes go, your attention goes.*

Do not focus them intensely like laser beams. Rather, use a gentle gaze and take in the entire object. Notice the creases, folds, color and other features, but do so passively, without any analysis or opinion forming. Look with a *sense of ease.* Have you ever been in the countryside, lying in a field, lazily looking up at the clouds? This is the kind of focus we're looking for at Level One.

This is very different from the way we look at our digital devices. When we look at a screen, the eyes have a hungry, absorbing, speedy quality to them, which you can actually feel if you pay close enough attention. Likewise, the mind that receives the images from the eyes feels speedy, tense, and grasping.

Intention

There is preparatory exercise called *The Wall* in chapter 9. That exercise comes into play now that you're trying to move this object. If you haven't read it yet or watched the related video[*], you should do so now before going further.

With your eyes looking at the object, have the intention that the object will move. Do not be concerned about which direction it will turn, or how fast. Keep it simple, only that the object will move.

Some people might suggest, "Just talk to it in your head, say 'Move!' over and over again!" I disagree with this advice. Language formation requires the use of the thinking aspect of awareness. This excess conceptualizing robs energy, weakening your intention's capacity to influence matter.

---

[*] Certain chapters contain web page addresses which have special videos and recordings specifically designed for readers of this book.

Instead, remember *The Wall* and the silent impulse you felt inside your mind during that exercise, the moment just before your body responded by moving.

Generate that same impulse now, and maintain it steadily. This is very subtle and difficult to describe with words, but if you practiced *The Wall* sufficiently, you will be able to relate to this guidance. You will be able to tell that the impulse is present and that you are keeping it steady, because there will be something that I can only describe as a *non-physical pressure* in your mind.

The word "sensation" isn't quite right since it's merely the *feeling of mental exertion*. It is not a type of physical strain. It's similar to the exertion you feel when trying to remember someone's name, or when you're trying to guess who's calling you when your phone rings and you don't recognize the number.

Think of the mental intention as the propulsion of your *will*. You are *willing* the object to turn. The problem with the word "will" is that it might tempt people to strain, and soon their faces will be bright red, their breathing will be forced, and their veins will be popping out of the skin. That's not our approach.

Look at the object and, from within your mind, tell it to move*. How does your mind feel when you do that? There is a subtle feeling that comes with the word "move." Try it a few more times, and get acquainted with that *feeling behind the word*. When you eat a piece of chocolate, the word "chocolate"

---

* Just for the purpose of this exercise.

Defy Your Limits   Sean McNamara

might arise in your consciousness, but that's not the actual flavor. And just as you're perfectly capable of tasting chocolate without repeating the word, you can intend the object to move without using the word "move."

Don't worry too much about perfecting this right now. It will come with time, and the other parts of the Level One instruction will help the object move while you learn more about your mind.

Approach

Slowly bring your hands toward the object. Don't be concerned if it is still spinning or wobbling because of air movement. When your hands are close enough, the energetic connection will change the behavior of the object.

Ideally the air in the room will be still, as will be the object. When a connection is established, it will be obvious because it will react through movement. If the object is moving because of air disturbance, you will know you have established a connection because it will either 1) stop moving suddenly, 2) reverse the direction of its movement, 3) increase or decrease its speed, or 4) change the *quality* of its movement, becoming smoother and more constant – *more intentional.*

If your hands get close enough to touch the object, stop. Instead, keep applying your attention and intention while you reverse your arm movement. Slowly widen your arms, noticing any reaction from the object while the distance between it and the hands increases.

If there was no response when you pulled your arms wide, keep repeating the process of approaching and backing away until you see the reaction.

You can watch an example of this exercise, including footage of the moment when the connection is made at: http://www.defyyourlimitsbook.com/beta.html

Testing distance

Once you see a reaction from the object, pause the movement of your hands. Keep your attention and intention (A&I)[*] on the object, and see how it behaves for a few moments. Does it continue to turn? Does it reverse direction? Does it freeze? If it freezes, do the ends of the object seem to be attracted to your palms, or have they settled in a more random direction?

There's no need to come to any conclusions. We're simply watching the behavior of the object and becoming familiar with it. An object moves differently depending on whether it's caused by air movement or telekinesis, and we need to learn the difference.

Slowly widen your arms while keeping your A&I on task. Move your hands away until the object stops responding. Does the connection seem to break right away? Or does it continue for some distance before it breaks?

---

[*] A&I will frequently be used as shorthand for attention and intention throughout the book.

Defy Your Limits   Sean McNamara

Pause your hands at the point of breaking the connection. Then slowly bring them closer again until the object responds anew. Hold them in that position and wait a few moments to watch the reaction again.

Repeat the process of backing the hands away until the connection is broken, and reconnecting as they draw closer again. Doing this will make you familiar with an object's typical response to your influence.

Applying the "Mind-Stopping Breath" technique for extra help

If after several attempts you still haven't established a connection, learn the *Mind-Stopping Breath* from chapter 12, and practice it several times.

How long should you try the above method (testing distance) before giving up and adding the breathing technique? I would recommend trying on a daily basis for one or two weeks. A day's session should last at least half an hour.

Begin by breathing in the prescribed manner, without doing anything else. Just sit there and practice the breathing. When you have relaxed your mind and body for perhaps five minutes, look at the object and apply your A&I for several more minutes.

While continuing your breathing, and applying your A&I, add the use of your hands by spreading your arms wide and slowly drawing them closer to the object, testing the distance as you learned earlier.

The only thing that has changed about this instruction is the addition of the Mind-Stopping Breath.

Move your hands closer then farther apart for several minutes while you repeat steady cycles of the breathing. Experiment with prolonging the held in-breath for longer than usual while applying you're A&I. *Look extra carefully during that moment and expect to see something happen.* Do the same with the held out-breath.

As much as this is about following instructions, it is also about experimentation. How long do you need to hold your breath? What if you filled your lungs with a little more air than usual, what would that do? What if you extended your bodily experience of relaxation out toward the object, combining it with your A&I?

Experimenting this way will not only increase your knowledge and confidence but it will also add a component of fun and curiosity to the process.

Transitioning to motionless hands

Spend several sessions widening and narrowing your arms and hands, looking for the sweet spot where the connection is made. It's possible that you won't be sure if the movement is the air moving or a telekinetic effect. Or perhaps the object still won't move in response to you.

If that is the case, change the instruction. Instead of "scanning" the distance with your arms, just place the hands a finger's distance away from either side of the object, and leave them there. Don't focus on your hands there, just drop them into that position, then ignore them. Apply your A&I to the object, relax your body and mind, and use the Mind-Stopping Breath. If you've already done the preparatory exercise called *The Refrigerator* from chapter 11, use it as well. Spend as many sessions as necessary doing this until you can influence the object.

This is as much about *giving it time* as it is about doing a technique. Just because it looks like nothing is happening *doesn't actually mean* nothing is happening. Your subconscious and subtle energy system need the time to learn, to *evolve*, so that you can do something you've never done before.

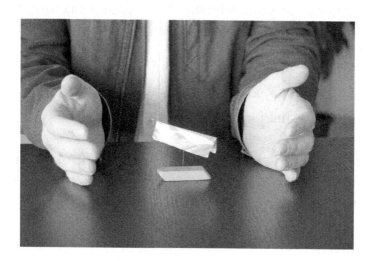

Gaining familiarity and control

After the first time the object responds to you, continue practicing until you develop some control over the object.

Level One

Here are some indications of the type of influence we're looking for:

- You will know with confidence the maximum distance your hands can be from the object while maintaining a connection.

- You will be able to tell the difference between when the object is moving due to the air in the room and when it's moving because of you.

- You will be able to affect the direction and speed of the movement. These manipulations will happen in response to your adjustment of your relaxation level and the intensity with which you apply the Mind-Stopping Breath.

- You will be able to affect the object this way while your hands are held in one position, unmoving.

Please be cautious when reading the word "control," though. In telekinesis, I like to call the object my *terrible dance partner*. It might go left when I want it to go right. It might respond to my direction late, several seconds after I gave it, not immediately.

This not about the object's ability to follow your command, exactly, it's about your ability to influence it. I leave it to the readers to determine if they're a good person to share a dance floor with. This work is sometimes subtle, other times, sloppy. It's more about *expression* and less about precision, like abstract art.

Influence establishes confidence and destroys doubt

Your inner non-believer and pseudo-skeptic may assert that the object is moving because of wind, static, or the heat of your hands. To counter those assertions, remember:

- Your hands were moving slowly enough to not generate the amount of air flow necessary to produce the movement (we assume that you were in a room with as little ambient air movement as possible).

- If static was present, it would actually *prevent* the kind of movement you observed.

- You were able to change the speed and direction of the object by changing your level of relaxation and your breathing pattern. Those were actions initiated by your mental intention. How could heat from the surface of your skin influence the object that way? How could wind change its direction and speed independently to produce that reaction?

To learn how static affects an object's motion, visit http://www.defyyourlimitsbook.com/beta.html

If you are unable to remove all doubt about those assertions within yourself, don't worry. Level Two will do a lot to reduce them significantly.

When you are ready, continue on to Level Two.

Level One

You can watch an example of Level One control here:
http://www.defyyourlimitsbook.com/beta.html

6. The Practitioner's State of Mind

As you continue on to the higher levels of training, which are more difficult, it will be important for you to establish a supportive state of mind within yourself.

Many successful people work with a mentor or a personal coach. One of the main roles of a coach is to help the person set goals, and to identify the necessary actions to meet and exceed them. They also help the person be accountable for executing those actions. By setting some expectations here, you will have an idea of how to keep yourself accountable for your training.

Telekinesis requires regular practice. Like playing the piano, oil painting, speaking a foreign language, and like succeeding in your career. It takes time and effort. When I used the words "Easiest" and "Fastest" in the title of my most popular online telekinesis video, it was the best and the worst thing I could have done. It was the best because I know how people search for "How To" videos. I wanted them to find mine, and with these search terms, they did. I also sincerely believe that the video did offer the easiest way to accomplish Level One.

It was also the worst thing I could have done because it gave the impression that telekinesis is generally easy and can be accomplished rapidly. I could tell from the online comments that when viewers didn't succeed right away, they thought something was wrong, and they quit too soon. I realized that it would only be those with passion, persistence, and motivation who would work on it long enough to succeed.

In light of that, the first expectation we should set from this point on is that *this will take work.*

The good news is that you will succeed at all four levels far quicker than I did because you have the method in this book. Still, it requires that you spend long periods of time in front of the object while it remains motionless. While you are sitting there, you'll relax your body, use the breathing technique, and manage various aspects of your consciousness. When all the conditions are right, an effect will be produced, and the object *will* move.

A watched pot never boils. This usually means that things seem to take far longer when we pay too much attention to them. Here, we'll take the opposite approach. You will sit and stare at that proverbial pot for a very time. You'll look at that pot as long as it takes for you to feel *like it's a part of you,* or that there's no distance between you.

There is a single indicator that you've done the required work, *it will move.* And it will do so without any warning at all, at least in the beginning. Knowing this ahead of time should help prevent a lot of future frustration and impatience. *Just because nothing seems to be happening doesn't mean that nothing is happening.*

My guess is that you already have a good degree of self-confidence and that you're optimistic about the training. Your inner believer and inner skeptic should be walking side by side in your consciousness, supporting your efforts.

Another expectation is that you understand that this is a *specific* training system, with specific results. Until you have succeeded through Level Four, I suggest not making any alterations or additions to the training method in this book. Give it a fair chance before becoming too experimental and adding new twists to the process.

You might be tempted to combine these instructions with others you gained somewhere else, or maybe you've made up some of your own. If you do that, you must acknowledge to yourself that you are no longer following the training method, that you are doing something different.

As I wrote earlier, there are many other ways to do telekinesis, and it is inevitable that you will create or discover them. I'm only suggesting you follow these instructions until you're successful, *and then* start exploring, using your new knowledge as a jumping off point.

There's a reason many teachers tell their students to forget everything they know before learning something new. It's usually what a student *thinks* they already know which confuses the instructions and ruins the process.

If you have never moved an object with your mind before, I now ask you to forget everything you think you know about telekinesis. The exception to this is for meditators. If you meditate regularly, no matter what technique you use, your familiarity with the various sensations, aspects, and movements of your mind will prove immensely helpful.

7. Introduction to the Preparatory Exercises

The next few chapters contain exercises to prepare you for Levels Two, Three, and Four*. If you continue your telekinesis practice beyond Level Four, what you learn through these exercises will be indispensable for you.

Telekinesis is about subtlety. Gentleness, relaxation and flow are desirable qualities for this process. Straining and forcing will work against you here. Patience wins every time, while rushing leads to failure. This subtlety not only concerns our approach with the techniques, but also how we access and stimulate the mental space and the physical body.

You may be tempted to pass over these exercises and go directly to Level Two. I recommend you don't. The exercises are simple to do, and will help you succeeded sooner. Each exercise offered here will empower your progress.

I will explain the purpose of each preparatory exercise below.

---

* If you have difficulty with Level One, these exercises will help with that one too.

Energy Follows Attention

This exercise will help you physically experience the principle that energy flows wherever you place your attention, where you focus. You'll combine your attention, intention, and breathing to stimulate energetic movement in your body. This experiment uses *sensation*.

After doing it several times, you will notice two important things:

- The steadier you hold your attention, the stronger and faster the effect is.

- It always *takes time* for the effect to accumulate, and for the sensation to build.

If you remember this when moving the telekinesis object, you'll understand why it does not immediately respond to your efforts. The steadier your *attention and intention* are, the sooner the effect will occur.

The Wall

Do you know what joy feels like in your mind? Or excitement, anger, and desire? How about feelings of avoidance or comfort?

How about intention? You know what the word "intention" means, or how it relates to taking action, but what I'm asking here specifically is if you know *how intention itself feels*?

The first purpose of this exercise is to become familiar with how intention feels in the mind. The second purpose is to feel the difference between intention and attention.

You've probably never isolated the mental factor of intention in your daily experience before. When you want to get something, you just get it. Want to go somewhere? You just go. It's an automatic aspect of living in a physical body, and we take it for granted.

In between an urge to move and its bodily response, there's *a silent impulse* coming from what we'll call your *nonconceptual mind*, the part of your mind that operates without language or ordinary thoughts.

For our purposes, *intention* is better described as a feeling than a thought. The exercise will help you experience what is quite difficult to describe with words here.

To differentiate between intention, attention and energy, imagine standing inside a strange building at night. The electricity goes out and you are surrounded by darkness. Let's say that your legs are the mental *factor of intention*, and since you happen to have a flashlight, the beam of light showing where to go is the *factor of attention*. The light shines on a doorway, and now your legs know where to take you. Without seeing the doorway, you would remain idle inside of that dark room. What is it that actually propels your legs? Your *energy*.

These are the fundamental concepts for this method. Intention, attention, and energy. You will learn to consciously direct your intention and attention toward the object.

Introduction to the Preparatory Exercises

The energy, however, *will move on its own*. It will respond to your attention and intention in a natural way. Remember the working hypothesis for this method, that *energy follows attention*.

The exercise *The Wall*, will help you draw the subtle strand of intention from the fabric of your mind. Once you're more familiar with it you'll be able to invoke it during your training sessions.

Spoonfuls

Your *will-power* is another required mental factor. Meditators rely on it in the moments when boredom, irritation or some other undesirable experience has arisen in their mind. In those moments, they can choose to end their session, get up, and go distract themselves with some other activity. Or, they can choose to stay, to continue on, and persevere. The will is not an emotional thing, though.

It's a silent force, similar to intention, which keeps you going in your originally intended direction regardless of any conflicting or distracting ideas that may have arisen. *Spoonfuls* is a basic exercise to illustrate the use of your will. Like intention, you will be exercising your will during your training sessions.

While your intention is directed to the object, your will-power will be applied toward *your own mind*. The will-power's purpose is to keep you on task and to deflate any urges to end a training session too soon due to boredom, impatience, and discouragement.

The Refrigerator

During my own early telekinesis development, I noticed two peculiarities that eventually helped me realize an important interaction between the silent nonconceptual mind and the *noisy thinking mind*.

The first one concerned something that would happen the moment I *gave up* trying to move the object. Sometimes I would spend thirty or forty minutes straight, looking at the object and trying everything I could do to move it. Then, exhausted and frustrated, I would decide to quit for the day. Immediately following that impulse to stop, the object would begin to turn.

This suggested that I was doing something wrong for 99% of the training session, and in that last second, when I decided to quit, I was finally doing *something right*.

The second peculiarity was that I tended to allow any kind of thinking to occur while I was applying my intention and attention toward the object. This included a lot of self-talk and analysis, trying to logically discern what was happening during a session. After failing to stimulate any movement, I would inevitably begin to daydream about completely unrelated topics. This was the natural outcome of boredom.

The daydreaming started happening more after I began employing the *Mind-Stopping Breath* while maintaining a good level of bodily relaxation. Relaxing my body also relaxed my mind.

Introduction to the Preparatory Exercises

58

Sometimes, the object would begin to move after I had shifted into daydreaming. Even though I was daydreaming, I still kept my gaze on the object and applied the silent intention for it to move.

Since I do not have access to an EEG machine (electroencephalogram), I can't say for certain if the moment of giving up and the period of daydreaming caused a shift in my brain's electrical activity. I strongly suspect that was the case, though.

A dominance of Beta level electrical activity is typical for the ordinary daytime thinking state. Alpha is typical for a relaxed mental state, which includes daydreaming and meditation. Theta also occurs in meditation as well as light sleep, and during energy healing*.

I hypothesize that in the brief moment of giving up on the experiment, my mind relaxed in a specific way. This level of relaxation was sufficient to allow the necessary energy to flow in order to influence the object. Also, whenever I allowed my thinking mind to depart into "La La Land," that also promoted relaxation. I believe that the Alpha and Theta states are optimal for the influence and flow of energy.

The combination of the special breathing technique and general relaxation with the passage of time will organically cause the prevalence of Alpha and Theta states during a training session.

---

* In the healer's mind, perhaps the patient's as well.

I have a second theory regarding the daydreaming effect. Let's create a mental model for the purpose of this discussion. Imagine that there is a line from you to the object. What part of "you" it originates from is not important for this conversation. Let's assume that your energy follows this line.

Let's add another component to that line - your *thinking mind*. In this model, both energy and conceptual mind can ride that line from you to the object.

While you're directing your attention to the object, simultaneously forming the intention for the object to turn, your energy is trying to *follow your attention along that line.*

Imagine that you're also having strong thoughts about the object, or about telekinesis, or about yourself while you're sitting there. Therefore, that noise in your mind is *crowding* the line. This causes the energy to become diluted, scattered, or otherwise weakened.

What if when we drift off into a daydream during an experiment, it actually *helps* to keep the line clear? Like throwing a stick to get a dog to run to a specific part of the yard, daydreaming is like sending our thinking mind somewhere else, *far away from the line* so that it doesn't get in the way. Without the noise, that energy flow would be more potent and steady.

I named this exercise *The Refrigerator* because the first time I realized the daydreaming effect, I had been wondering what was inside of my refrigerator. I was in the middle of a session, and the object hadn't moved yet. Distracted and hungry, I visualized the interior of the fridge and scanned my image for food items like cheese and eggs.

It was in that moment of distraction when the object finally began to turn, as if suddenly released from an invisible restraint.

Since then, during these sessions when the object remained still for far too long, I would recreate that effect by purposely imagining walking to the fridge, opening the door, and seeing what food items were stored on each shelf. I still kept my attention and intention on the object, however.

According to our mental model above, this technique allowed the energy to flow better and/or stronger.

The Mind-Stopping Breath

As mentioned earlier, we can affect our minds by changing our bodily state. By adopting and modifying breath work from techniques I had learned before, I began to practice what I found to be a reliable method for telekinesis. I had initially used it solely for relaxing the body. Regular practice revealed that different phases of the breath could affect the *mind* in different ways.

More interesting, though, was that when I was firmly entrained* with an object, the cycle of inhalations, exhalations, and pauses coincided with the clockwise and counter-clockwise movement of the object. Certain phases of the breath could also stop the movement altogether.

---

* See *Entrainment with the Object* in *Level Two*

This relationship between the breathing and the direction of movement leads me be to believe that telekinesis is an effect of energy. Consider Yin-Yang theory from the Taoist tradition of China. Yin represents qualities like softness, darkness, downward movement, and the night. Yang represents qualities of hardness, light, upward movement, and daytime.

In Taoism and Chinese Medical Theory, everything that exists has a yin and yang component. They are natural complements to each other since everything exists through the progression of cycles. Day becomes night, which makes way for the next day. Birth gives way to death, making room for the seeds of new life to sprout. Blood is sent from the heart to the tips of our limbs in an outward, *yang* movement. Then that deoxygenated blood is returned to the heart by the venous system, a *yin* movement. As we inhale, we *draw in* fresh oxygen, yin. On the exhale, we *release* carbon dioxide, yang.

Entrained with an object at Level Two and beyond, I inhale, and it turns one direction. I pause, lungs filled to capacity, and my mind flickers for a moment. The object pauses its turn. Then I exhale, and the object turns in the opposite direction. I see this as evidence of the ying-yang nature of breathing and its influence on energy and movement.

A word of caution, however. *The breathing technique does not replace the need for using attention and intention.* Since those mental factors are subtle and the breathing is not, it can be easy to ignore the mind's role and rely solely on breathing in the hopes of success.

A balance must be struck so that all the key parts of the technique are applied together, leaving none idle. Otherwise

Introduction to the Preparatory Exercises

you'll find yourself breathing without success. The resulting stress will tighten your mind into a knot. Your body will respond accordingly. With the relaxation sabotaged, the inevitable tension will block the flow of energy. Don't overuse the breathing technique.

8. Exercise: Energy Follows Attention

Go to a quiet room where no one will disturb you. Any self-consciousness can prevent you from placing your attention on the intended object.

Sit down, and place your hands wherever they can rest comfortably, for instance in your lap or on your abdomen. Close your hands into soft fists, but choose one index finger and leave it extended.

You may either look at your finger with your eyes, or close your eyes and simply feel your finger from tip to base.

Can you feel the very tip of your finger? Take a few moments paying attention only to the very tip of your finger, and feel what the experience is like in that specific location.

After a few moments, move your focus to the joint closest to your finger nail. What does that section feel like? Again, give it a few moments. Simply pay attention and notice that *over time new and stronger sensations arise.*

Now move on to the middle knuckle of your finger, and do the same thing. Are the sensations similar to or different than the sensations in the other parts of your finger?

Pay attention to your whole finger for a couple of minutes, can you feel its entirety?

Now I'll introduce another working hypothesis. Let's assume that energy is not only inside our body but all around, in the environment that surrounds us. Various traditions believe that this energy can be transported by the air, among other ways. When we inhale, we draw this energy into ourselves. These traditions also teach that the energy can enter directly through the skin, especially if we intend it to. Keeping this in mind, continue the exercise.

Relax your body exactly where you are sitting. Allow your breath to become slower and fuller. You'll notice when this is happening by how much your abdomen expands on the inhale. Breathe slowly so that you feel your abdomen stretch out a bit while your lungs fill with air. Then exhale naturally.

Breathing this way, place your attention back on your finger. On the inhale, imagine that energy is entering your finger through the skin that surrounds it.

Then, imagine that energy is coming into it through your forearm, wrist and hand, moving into the base of your finger. It's perfectly acceptable to *pretend* that this is happening.

Pretending is a way of visualizing, and it's also a vehicle for one's intention.

As you inhale, pretend or imagine that a cool, white light is touching and passing through the skin and entering your finger. As you exhale, simply relax and continue to feel the sensations in your finger. On the next inhale, imagine this cool, white light coming in to your finger.

Exhaling, notice the increased sensitivity in your finger. You may even feel a vivid quality, as if your finger has come to life, feeling more refreshed and sparkly.

You have been paying steady attention to your finger and as a result, ignoring most of the rest of your body and the environment. Perhaps you were able to pay less attention to your thinking as well, while remaining in a *feeling* state.

Simply by adding the visualization, the energy came and infused your finger. The new sensations of vividness, presence, and brightness in your finger are hallmarks of fresh energy stimulating the body.

This concept is easy to experience right away. It is also something that you can improve over time.

You may also try this exercise by following along with my audio guided instructions which you can listen to here: http://www.defyyourlimitsbook.com/iota.html

There, you can also listen to a guided meditation to bring energy into your whole body. You might find it relaxing and enjoyable. Doing it once in a while will undoubtedly help you with your telekinesis practice.

Exercise: Energy Follows Attention

A Brief Note on Healing Potential with this Exercise

Although I'll address healing more toward the end of the book, I'd like to mention it here because of its relationship to the principle *Energy Follows Attention*.

Do you have an injury to your body, or an area of illness? You can apply the above instructions to draw energy to that body part, thus aiding in healing and in pain reduction[*]. The particular body part may initially feel more sore when you start the practice, but know that you are just increasing your awareness of how it really feels.

This method requires that rather than blocking out a sensation, you open your mind to it. With practice, you'll notice an increased ability to allow any discomfort to arise, and a lessening of your resistance against it. If you stay with the process, the breath-work and attention will cause a shift in your experience of that pain. In the right circumstances, healing may be accelerated and the pain abated.

---

[*] Check first with your qualified healthcare professional if you have any questions or concerns, or before changing your treatment or medication plan.

9. Exercise: The Wall

Go to a wall in your home or office and stand facing it, one or two paces away.

Close your eyes and breathe easily, the same way you did with the previous exercise, "Energy Follows Attention." Let your neck and shoulders relax. The softer you can make your body, the easier it will be for you to pay attention to what's happening within.

Are you having a lot of thoughts? Are you thinking about being somewhere else? Do you feel present in the room, or is your mind somewhere else?

Continue breathing for a couple more minutes, inviting your body to soften and relax even further. Notice how nice it feels to do that.

After a while, notice that you are more present in the room, that you're more in touch with your body, and your mind is a little less full of distracting thoughts.

In a moment, you will open your eyes, lift your arm and touch your fingertips to the wall. Before you do, pay special attention to all the subtle feelings in your mind. You might imagine that your mind is like outer space, black and mostly empty. Once in a while, you feel, see or hear words, emotions, or things you can't describe popping in and out of that empty darkness.

When you are ready, simply open your eyes, *reach out and touch the wall.* After you touch it, you can let your arm come down again.

Think back to the moment just before you opened your eyes to see the wall and move your arm. What happened in your mind? What did you feel? Did anything occur in that black empty space? *We are looking for that feeling of impulse, your intention.* It's a little blip, a little movement, a shift, and it's very quick. As soon as it came and went, your eyes and body obeyed its command.

Try it again, this time paying much closer attention to what's happening in your mind. Close your eyes, relax your body, and as you decide to touch the wall (which includes opening your eyes to see it and lifting your arm), *notice that subtle event in your mind.*

If it helps, you might say the word "Now!" within your mind and then pay attention to the next moment, the moment *just before you physically respond.*

Do it again, and this time after you touch the wall, intend to keep your fingers pressed against it for a few moments. While they're touching the wall, *keep intending* to feel the texture of the wall. *When you decide* to let your arm back down, try to capture the *feeling of your intention* when it arises in your mind.

I would also recommend pressing your fingers against the wall for a few moments without expressly using your intention. Just let your subconscious do it for you while you think about other things. You could try adding up all the numbers of your birthday's month, day and year. Or think about a problem you're having at work. Then return your awareness to your fingers, and *feel a fresh intention arise when you decide* to let your arm down.

The purpose of this is to show you that just because your body is in a held position doesn't mean that your intention was necessarily activated.

This will be important later when you realize half-way through a telekinesis session that your eyes may be physically looking at the object, but your intention has vaporized, leaving your energy idle and directionless.

You might want to spend ten or fifteen minutes repeating this exercise. Each time, you will pick up little hints of intention arising in your mind. You'll become familiar with *how it feels to invoke the feeling of intention.* While you're pressing your fingertips against the wall, stay in tune with the intention which keeps them there. When you decide to let your arm down, notice how a *new experience of intention* arises in your mind just before your arm responds.

Try this exercise by following along with my audio guided instructions which you can listen to here:
http://www.defyyourlimitsbook.com/iota.html

Exercise: The Wall

10. Exercise: Spoonfuls

You will need the following supplies:

- Two medium sized bowls. Each should be able to contain five cups of uncooked rice.
- A teaspoon.
- Five cups of uncooked rice.

Pour five cups of rice into one of the bowls, and leave the other one empty. Set both bowls in front of you while you're seated at a table. Place one bowl toward the left, further left than where your left shoulder reaches. Place the other bowl to the right, also a little beyond where your right shoulder reaches. Now the two bowls are significantly spaced apart.

Remember that the goal of this exercise is to experience your will-power in action. The more bored, disinterested, or irritated you become, *the better*. If you want to quit the exercise half-way through, that will be the prime opportunity to exercise your will and feel what that it's like to continue the exercise that way.

Before continuing, make the commitment that you will see the whole exercise through to the end, at least once. The sense of commitment is crucial for activating your will.

Scoop the rice from one bowl to the other, one teaspoon full at a time. The rule is that you can't overfill the spoon so that it spills grains of rice. You also can't move at a speed that causes you to spill any.

Continue until one bowl is empty and the other is full. Again, what we're looking for here is something akin to subtle exasperation. You may even have the thought, "Ok, I get the point! I understand what you're trying to show me, so I'm just going to stop now and save myself some time." What you must do at that point is to let your will *take over*.

Your will can function to keep you going even though your noisy thinking mind is coming up with reasons why it's ok to quit before finishing. Knowing the point of the lesson is *not the same as going through it*.

Like intention, will has its own texture in the mind. For me, it feels plain, solid, uninteresting, and unemotional. It feels removed and independent of my emotional self, so it doesn't respond to my inner complaints. It keeps moving forward with the process until it's done, while another part of me whines and gripes. Understanding that both of these can operate at the same time, you can place more importance on the will and *keep going*.

In this manner, you'll keep scooping up the rice slowly to fill the other bowl, over and over again, even if you don't want to any more. As you do, experience the texture of your will inside your mind. What does will *feel* like?

Exercise: Spoonfuls

11. Exercise: The Refrigerator

Recall the exercise, "Energy Follows Attention", where you paid attention to your finger while imagining energy coming into it with every inhale. Spend a couple of minutes doing the exercise now until your finger feels tingly, alive, fresh, velvety, or whatever words you would use to describe your energized finger.

Continue paying attention to your finger while breathing with the intention of filling it with energy. *At the same time,* use your imagination and see yourself opening your refrigerator.

Your mind might flicker between being aware of your finger and seeing your refrigerator in your imagination. It might not be easy to think of both things at the same time. That's fine. The most important thing is to relax and not be concerned about getting this right or doing it perfectly. That kind of attitude causes stress, which prevents anything at all from happening.

Stay with the finger exercise a few moments before trying again. When you're ready, see yourself opening the fridge door. While you're looking inside your visualized fridge, continue feeling your finger while noticing your inhale and exhale.

It can feel like the mind is going in two directions. Better said, it's like the mind is being split. Perhaps it's similar to how it feels when learning to play the piano with both hands at the same time.

The nonconceptual part of your mind is feeling your finger, and that attention acts like a beacon, calling the surrounding energy to it. Meanwhile the noisy thinking mind is off in your memory of your kitchen, trying to recall what's inside the fridge right now, and distinguishing between articles of food. This part of the mind has *stepped away from the line of energy.*

Please do not spend too much time on this exercise trying to perfect it. Its purpose is simply to show you a new way to work with your mind. You'll have plenty of time to practice it while you're actually trying to make an object move during the telekinesis sessions.

You'll be using this technique from time to time whenever you sense that your noisy thinking mind is preventing your energy from flowing to the object.

Exercise: The Refrigerator

12. Special Technique: The Mind-Stopping Breath

This instruction is given in four phases so that you can learn it piece by piece, comfortably. You will know the complete technique when you use all four together in a cycle of breathing.

Phase 1

If you are slouching, the first step is to sit up straight because when you slouch, everything in your torso becomes compressed. By sitting up, you're making room for your internal organs and abdominal muscles to move naturally.

Place both of your hands on your belly. This will help you feel if you are breathing in a complete manner or not.

Inhale, and notice which parts of your torso move. Exhale naturally. Did your chest expand, did your shoulders rise? Did your belly move at all?

Inhale again, taking in a slightly deeper breath than last time. See if you can keep your shoulders and chest relaxed, and accentuate the feeling of your belly expanding outward. Feel your belly pressing against your hands.

The feeling beneath your hands will resemble holding a balloon as it inflates with air. Exhale when you need to. You should then feel your belly collapsing slightly as you release air from your lungs.

The reason your belly expands on the inhale is because you are now using the main breathing muscle, the *thoracic diaphragm*. You can visualize the diaphragm as a wide, flat muscle that sits just underneath your lungs. The reason your lungs fill with air when you inhale is that when the diaphragm contracts, it extends downward, which lengthens the lungs and chest cavity. This draws air into them.

Your belly moves forward and out of the way to make room for the downward contraction of the diaphragm. This makes it feel as if it were expanding. As I wrote earlier, this type of breathing stimulates relaxation in the body and mind, in large part because you are taking in more oxygen than you would when breathing shallowly.

Phase 2

Inhale again in the same way, and as you exhale, see if you can gently push out as much air from your lungs as possible. Gently pull your abdominal muscles in, as if to squeeze out any air that might still be inside. I repeat the word "gently" here because you shouldn't strain or cause yourself to become light headed. If that happens, stop immediately. We're only looking for a thorough exhalation, nothing more.

While exhaling, let go of any physical tension throughout your whole body. Let your hands, arms and legs become soft

Special Technique: The Mind-Stopping Breath

76

and heavy. Let your neck be loose. Try invoking words like "releasing," "letting go," and "melting" as you exhale.

Phase 3

Inhale as in Phase 1, and then pause for several moments before exhaling. Don't hold the breath by contracting your throat or upper chest, like tying a knot in a balloon valve.

You'll know if you are doing this because your belly will contract inwardly at the same time. Instead, simply keep holding your belly out, extended. This instruction is a way of keeping your diaphragm contracted downward and the space in the torso lengthened. This is a more relaxed way of holding the breath in. After a few moments, exhale normally.

Even though there is some level of effort involved in holding the belly out, try to keep the rest of your body soft, loose, and released as you did in Phase 2.

Phase 4

After taking a few normal breaths, exhale completely as you did in Phase 2, and then pause for a few moments before inhaling again. Keeping the air out is a little easier than holding it in the way you did in Phase 3. To keep the air out, hold your abdominal muscles in. Again, don't clench your throat. When you need to, inhale normally and continue breathing naturally.

A complete cycle of breathing

Inhale, extending your belly out and filling your lungs completely, but without strain.

Hold the breath for several seconds by keeping the belly extended.

Exhale slowly, and at the end of the breath pull in your abdominal muscles to squeeze out any remaining air.

Hold the exhale and keep your lungs empty for several seconds until you need to inhale again.

Repeat the cycle with another full inhalation, going through all four phases while feeling relaxed as possible.

How this technique affects the conceptual mind

Our breathing has a direct effect on our body, our energy, and our mental activity. Do several cycles of breathing now, and see if you can notice something subtle. While you're inhaling, pay attention to the space in your mind.

Notice the mental activity. Are there lots of thoughts, or a few, or a medium amount? Are they moving quickly, or is it just one thought that's sitting there? What do you experience when you look within your mind?

As you fill up with air completely and move to the phase of holding in the breath, do you notice any change in your mind?

Special Technique: The Mind-Stopping Breath

This is very subtle, so it might take a few rounds for you to see what I'm indicating here.

It's like a flicker, a pause, or a shift somewhere inside. It may even feel slightly physical in your skull, or like your eyes lost track of what you were looking at for just a millisecond. It's an interruption of your thinking pattern, an ultrafast moment of peace.

Try a few more rounds of the breath and see if you can pinpoint that moment. You may never be quite sure if you've found it, or whether what you believe it to be is what I'm talking about. It's that subtle. The important thing is for you *tune in to your mental space*, while relaxed, as you're holding in the breath for a few moments.

This is important because this is a way to *initiate the flow of energy*. It is possible that during your telekinesis session, the first movement will begin while you've quieted your noisy thinking mind during the brief period of holding the breath.

Now try looking at your mind at the end of an exhalation, while you're keeping your lungs empty and your abdominal muscles pulled in. It's a similar experience to when you're holding the air in, but not exactly. In my experience it feels slightly different. Regardless, sometimes it is at this point of the breathing cycle when the object will begin to move for you. Experimentation over time will be necessary to see what works best for you.

Special opportunities by using this technique

The object may begin its movement at any phase of your breathing cycles. Yet the top and the bottom of each cycle present a special opportunity.

Imagine that a half-hour has passed and still no movement has occurred. You begin using the "Mind-Stopping Breath" as I've taught it up to this point. Several cycles later, it still hasn't moved.

What I would recommend at that point is to experiment in this way – hold your breath far longer than you normally would. Be careful not to strain. Just stretch your comfort zone, and hold on a little longer. The end of this moment is when the object may finally begin its movement.

Then exhale, and remember to keep your body and mind relaxed as you do so. If you tighten up from excitement at seeing the object move, it might stop the effect because excitement is a form of tension. If your mind starts flooding with thoughts and emotions, that noise will dampen the energetic flow.

Try doing the same at the bottom of the cycle, holding your belly out and keeping your lungs empty for a few seconds before inhaling again. Remember to keep your eyes, attention and intention on the object the whole time while you work with the breath.

In the beginning, you'll need to let yourself go back to breathing normally after a brief attempt in order to catch your breath. This is normal and you should do so. Only when

Special Technique: The Mind-Stopping Breath

you've normalized your breathing and you feel comfortable should you go back to the breathing technique.

With regular practice and the passage of time you'll become proficient at breathing this way continuously for long periods.

> You may also learn this exercise by watching the video here: http://www.defyyourlimitsbook.com/alpha.html

13. Working with the Eyes

Over the months when I developed myself from Level Two through Level Four, I realized that there was a peculiar relationship between my eyes and the object. You already know through this training that the eyes are the directors of one's attention. They do more than just that, though.

They listen.

I'm going to explain a subtle concept now which you may have never heard before. It may be challenging to imagine what I'm going to describe here, but by reading it now, you'll be able to identify it while it's happening.

During the remaining levels, there will be long periods of stillness before the object begins to move. You'll begin a session by following the instructions for *entraining* with the object, which include noticing all the visual details of it, the wrinkles, the color, and the rest. After you feel more connected to the object, you will naturally abandon the process of picking out its small details.

Your eyes will seem to take a more passive approach to looking at the object. They might behave more like open windows, and the object will simply be an image appearing within them. Your attention and intention at this point will be firmly established, and you may even feel a strong sense of mental connection from within your consciousness. Your eyes will also feel far more physically relaxed than they did at the beginning.

Imagine that your eyes are more centered on the left side of the object. Or perhaps one end is angled closer to your body, and your eyes naturally rest on that part. The nearby corner is a clear image while the opposite one is more a part of the fuzzy background imagery.

Then a silent impulse arises, *almost like an invitation,* to move your vision across the object's surface and rest on the opposite end. You accept the invitation and shift your attention to a different section of the object. Moments later, it begins to move. Why did that happen?

Earlier, I suggested that the eyes *listen.* The reason I put it this way is because that silent impulse seems like the object is telling my eyes where they need to go. I am not saying that the object is actually talking to me, of course.

I think the message actually comes from the subconscious mind. It knows what we're trying to do, and it's asking the body to make the necessary adjustment with the eyes in order to draw the energy more effectively.

More provocatively, what if the energy that is flowing into the object is not only capable of moving the object, but of *retrieving information about it and communicating that information back to the mind*?

An important question is whether the energy we've been talking about throughout the book is something distinct from consciousness or not. Are they really two different things? Like the particle state and the wave state of light, could energy and consciousness simply be two different behaviors of the same thing?

There is another action your eyes may take during a long, quiet session. They may drift a bit, centering just off one edge of the object. Their focus might float just over the top edge, underneath, or beside the object. Your A&I is still fully engaged upon the object, no longer requiring the use of the eyes in the same way. Your mind knows the object is there, you still intend to move it.

The image still appears, but somewhere off center, as a peripheral image.

When you notice that this has occurred, don't worry, and do not rush to center the image in your visual field. Just notice that you're still paying attention and applying the rest of the techniques. If several minutes later there still isn't any movement, you might "freshen up" your session by taking a brief break, and then re-focusing your eyes on it and re-entraining with the object.

This "eye drift" is a sign that you've done a great job of relaxing your body and mind during the session. Remember, the more relaxed you are, the better your energy flows.

The relaxation also lets the experience of attention and intention stand out in your awareness, so that you can really tell that they're engaged. It's more difficult to perceive those mental factors when the mind is tense and turbulent with other mental activity like self-talk and theorizing.

A note from the ancient spiritual practice "Togal"

There is an ancient meditative practice that many people today encounter through the Tibetan lineages of Dzogchen. These teachings and practices, translated as "The Great Perfection" were known long before Buddhism came to Tibet.

One particular practice from that tradition[*] called "Togal[**]" involves using the eyes to perceive light from various natural sources like the sun, moon, and candle light. It also includes complete immersion into darkness for long periods of time.

The eyes have a unique function during these particular meditations. Their role seems to be curiously similar to how we use the eyes during telekinesis. The description is so intriguing that I include it here for your consideration.

The following is from *Primordial Grace, Earth, Original Heart, and the Visionary Path of Radiance.* It was written by Robert and

---

[*] Other cultures and traditions have also developed ways to meditate with light over the millennia.
[**] Usually translated as "leap over" or "direct crossing".

Defy Your Limits   Sean McNamara

Rachel Olds*, who are well-experienced practitioners of that path. Their text offers the clearest and most understandable introduction to this path available in the English language.

From the chapter *Heartlamp of the Eyes***

"The fluid receptive nature of the eyes and their ability to perceive light is called the *heartlamp of the eyes*. The eye has a natural fluid power that reaches out and connects with what it sees, and has sometimes been called a water lasso for that reason. The eyes can meet, hold, push, or pull at need. If this power is guided by the mind, the mind grabs onto what the eyes see, and pulls it back into itself and interprets it in ways that reinforce perceptions upholding separate identity. The eyes can also be used more purely, to connect with and relate, and with this more open use of the eyes, you bond and blend with the visions as they arise."

I don't mean to suggest in any way that telekinesis is related to Togal. However, the eyes and their role in consciousness and perception as described in both Togal and telekinesis makes for a provocative comparison.

---

* Many thanks to Rachel and Robert Olds for sharing their knowledge and experience of Togal.
** Grateful acknowledgment is made for permission from Robert Olds and Heart Seed Press to reprint this excerpt.

Working with the Eyes

14. Level Two*

I will begin this section with good news and bad news. Remember that at this level, you will keep your object covered with a glass container.

The good news is that once you have succeeded at Level Two, you will have dealt your self-doubt a hefty blow and your telekinetic ability will be far stronger than it was at Level One.

The bad news is that at the beginning, you may become convinced that Level One wasn't really telekinesis. You might stare at the glass barrier and begin to think that there's no way you could actually move the object with your mind.

You may start to think this way because in your first session at Level Two, it's possible that nothing will happen. No movement whatsoever. It will take more sessions to succeed at Level Two than it did at Level One.

Don't worry. You can, and *will* succeed. It's just a matter of working with the ideas in your mind, and putting in the time.

---

* Estimated time for success: one to four weeks

As you sit there in frustration some of the following thoughts might arise:

Look at it! It's inside that thing, and I'm on the outside. We can't touch! How on earth am I supposed to do this?

Was I really foolish enough to think that I could move something over there with my mind?

It's sitting like a rock! And my thoughts aren't physical, they're nothing! How could they ever affect a physical object?

I'm mentioning these thoughts now before you begin so that you can deal with them right away. I know them intimately. They haunted me during every session, every week, every month until I was successful. I exercised my will and stayed the course.

My faith in what I believed possible was stronger than my insecurity and doubt. You can have that same faith in yourself.

It was helpful for me to realize that I could continue my regular training sessions and simply *expect these thoughts to arrive.* I let them have a small corner of my mind to hang out in, instead of trying to force them out. Meanwhile, I got to work, paying attention to the object.

Now that you know what to expect, we can begin.

Level Two

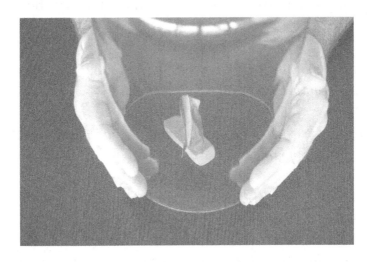

Using the glass container

Sit at a height that allows you to clearly see the object through the glass. If the top edge of the container falls into your line of sight, it will deform the image as it appears through the glass. Because you are depending on your use of sight to direct your attention, it's important that you have as clear and unmodified image as possible during the training session.

Arms and Hands

Rest your arms comfortably on the table, so that your palms and fingers are gently placed against the sides of the glass container. Your hands should not press against the glass, only remain *gently in contact with it*. They shouldn't move in any way nor should the container slide or shift.

Eyes

As in Level One, apply a gentle gaze upon the object. Pay attention to every detail, then look at its entirety. Completely ignore the glass. Look past it, ignoring any reflections or smudges. Pretend it's not even there.

Intention

Just as in Level One, feel that subtle movement of mind, that subtle pressure, as you *will* the object to move through your attention and intention.

Breathing

Begin regular cycles of the *Mind-Stopping Breath* while maintaining your A&I.

Be prepared to sit with the object at least a half-hour at a time. Even if you become distracted or agitated, do your best to stay present with it. Remember that energy accumulates over time.

Even if it appears as if nothing is happening, trust that a connection between you and the object is being established. What is most important during these long periods of non-movement is that you keep your attention (eyes) and intention (will/mind) on the object as *consistently* as you can.

During each session, spend the first fifteen minutes following the above instructions. Consider this a period of simply accumulating energy into the object. After fifteen minutes, you can experiment in the following ways:

Try extending the top and bottom of your breath cycles once or twice every few minutes. These are moments when the object could respond to your intention.

Periodically apply the technique from the training exercise *The Refrigerator*. It's good to use it when your mind has become especially noisy and when you're experiencing a lot of self-talk, theorizing, and analysis about the object and this experiment.

Send the thinking mind out of the room, send it away to see what's in the fridge. Give your intention and energy some breathing room. Just like with the *Mind-Stopping Breath*, shifting this way may be create the moment when the object begins to move.

It's not necessary to separate the mind like this during an entire session. Rather, use *The Refrigerator* when you suspect that you're overthinking or feeling any kind of excess tension in your mind. If you're trying to *think* the object into moving, you've departed from the instructions.

We want to *feel* the object into moving. Take a break, relax, and review the instructions for Level One and Two. You may notice that you are doing things that weren't part of the instructions, which could be getting in the way. With this kind of telekinesis, more is usually not better.

Entrainment with the Object

The word "entrainment" has different meanings depending on its context. According to the online encyclopedia *Wikipedia*, in engineering it is defined as "the entrapment of one substance by another substance." In physics, "the process whereby two interacting oscillating systems assume the same period." In biomusicology, "the synchronization of organisms to an external rhythm."

The notions of one substance affecting another and of two systems matching the same rhythm give a sense of the relationship that we form with the object. We're not talking about a measurable interaction though. Rather, this is what the experience of telekinesis *feels like* beginning at Level Two and going beyond. We're tuning in to the object by shifting our mental and bodily experience.

The first step to developing the relationship is noticing how your mind experiences the object as being some distance away from *you*, your body and mind. Actually, we assume that separation from our whole external world. We're here, and everything else is *out there*, distant in space. To develop a relationship with the object, you need to soften that unspoken belief of your separation from it.

In a coming chapter, *Mental Models and Basic Principles*, the working hypothesis is that when we perceive through our physical senses, we separate from reality. We'll learn that what we perceive in our brains is only an electrochemical *translation* of a signal passed through the nervous system.

Level Two

The eye itself is only capable of perceiving a select portion of the electromagnetic spectrum, so it's not seeing everything that's out there. Our brain creates a model of the external world, and part of that model is the sense of separateness between you and the object. Simply reflecting on this idea can be enough to open your mind to unseen possibilities.

In our case, this information can help us feel more connected to the object. We no longer need to believe that we're truly separate because there's enough evidence to suggest that things are different than they appear. Maybe we're more connected than we thought. Maybe we, and those things we consider *out there* and apart from us, are really all *one thing*.

The "maybe" is enough, we don't need to depend on proof from the world of physics or believe what various spiritual traditions have to say. Your *experience* of moving an object from a distance will give you adequate data for your initial consideration.

To close the distance between us and the object, there are special ways to perceive it. First, notice the details. Look at its shape, color, and texture. Notice the creases, wrinkles and angles. There's no need to memorize anything, just paying close attention to it is enough. Look at the edges of the object, the dividing line between it and its surrounding space.

Next, imagine what the object feels like. If you can't recall what tinfoil feels like, take it off the needle and spend a few minutes feeling it carefully with your fingers. Notice its temperature, the smoothness, and how the flat portion feels different from when you run your finger along its fine edge. How heavy does it feel?

While you're holding it in your hand, you might as well take a few whiffs of it and see if it has an odor of any kind. It might be subtle, but it's there. What's it like? Touch your tongue to it and get a sense of its flavor.

Place it back on the needle and cover it with the glass container. Return your hands to their position and begin applying your A&I. At the same time, bring to mind all your sense memories that you just created, feeling, tasting and smelling it. Keep your eyes on it and continue to appreciate the details.

Let's assume that when you did Level One, you weren't perceiving the object the way you will now after reading the instruction above. You regarded it as only an image some distance away from you. With these new instructions, your perception will widen, adding a fuller dimension to the object. Your *idea* of the object will have more texture, more to experience, and this will provide something more for your intention and energy to *come in contact with.*

As you continue applying your A&I toward the object in this more intimate way, the quality of separation and distance will weaken.

Consider how you regard your own hand. Hold your arm out straight. Does it seem far away from you? If you tend to be a logical person you might say "Yes!" because your eyes are up here and your hand is out there. If you're more of an intuitive type, or feeling-related, you'll probably respond with "No, it doesn't seem far away from me at all, it *is* me, or a part of me. It's in the same place *I am.*"

Level Two

The second person is communicating the same experience of relationship that we want to develop with the object. We want to feel like the space between the object and us, as well as the object, *are a part of us*, connected with us.

As with many aspects of telekinesis, it's better not to overthink this concept. Let time do the work instead. You will feel more connected to the object near the end of a long session than you do at the beginning.

You will also feel more connected to the object after several weeks of looking at it than you do after only a couple of days. All you need to do is show up on a regular basis and apply the looking, breathing, and the A&I instructions.

One day you might notice that the object just seems to be more a part of you, or your mind. It'll almost feel as if it would move the way your hand does, in response to a mental impulse. Or it may lack that subtle quality of separateness, the out-there-ness. Remember, this experience is more of a feeling tone in the mind than anything else.

The following scenario may help describe this experience. Assume that in the beginning you behaved as if your consciousness was centered in your head, looking out into the world through the windows of your eyes. They saw the object *out there*. During repeated training sessions, your consciousness began to feel like it had extended beyond the boundary of your head, occupying the space in between you and the object.

The sense of *you* felt expanded beyond your body. You even had moments when that sense of you *included* the object. It's as if your consciousness had expanded out across the entire distance and enfolded the object into its own space.

When you have the experience described above, you may begin to sense that the connection is almost strong enough so that when you gently push and pull your consciousness along that space, the object will be moved by it. This may or may not be related to how telekinesis actually works, but if you begin to feel this, or any similar experience, then it indicates that you have established a good degree of entrainment with it.

The only way to observe the entrainment of course is by its effect, by witnessing the motion of the object. It's just like the wind. You can't see it, but you know it's there because the trees are swaying and the clouds are floating across the horizon. It is also like love, you can't see it but you know its presence by how you feel inside, by your emotions and physical sensations. You must pay attention to *yourself* as much as to the object

There isn't any single thing we could call "the telekinetic mechanism." Perhaps it's a culmination of physical and mental conditions in the practitioner which produces an observable effect in the object. We must take it further though, because it's not just about us. We have to consider the conditions within the spatial distance, the environment, and of the object itself. *Their* conditions change too, since they are inherent aspects of the experiment.

Everything is connected; therefore everything is affected.

Level Two

Are we actually parts of a greater whole? Different spiritual traditions say that this is so, and some scientists, those courageous enough to explore beyond the known world, are looking into it. Perhaps telekinesis and practitioners like you can become a helpful voice in those conversations.

Micro-movements, Harbingers of Success

Know that full movement is around the corner once you perceive *micro-movements*. There are two kinds.

The first kind occurs within your mind. I have to use the word "mind" loosely here, because we have the mind that receives sensory input from organs like our eyes, and there is the mind that translates that input into colorful images. Another part of our mind combines concepts like names, labels, opinions, and past experiences with the raw images.

One aspect of mind receives signals from our taste buds in the mouth and our chemoreceptors inside the nose. Another aspect evokes the raw taste of chocolate in our consciousness. The third aspect of mind starts churning out thoughts, like the words "chocolate" and "delicious."

Please remember that I'm using *mental models* to share concepts with you throughout this training method. Biologists, neuroscientists, psychologists, and traditions like Buddhism have far more intricate explanations for how the arising of experience occurs in consciousness.

There are moments during a session when you will have been steadily looking at the unmoving object, and *your inner image of the object* will seem to move. It may or may not appear as a turn on the needle. It could just be a *feeling of motion*, but without seeing it. I frequently experience subtle, ultra-brief sensations of sinking, dizziness, or disorientation when this happens. The heaviness can occur in my head, chest, or belly.

Again, these sensations come and go very quickly, and it is only because of the quiet stillness of a telekinesis session that a person would even notice those shifts.

I've tried to record close-up video of the object while experiencing this internal micro-movement, because I haven't been completely sure of what I was perceiving. Was it really moving, or was it just in my head?

After recording these sessions, I'd play the video on a large screen to verify the movement. Perplexed, I observed none. Why was I perceiving motion in my mind, while nothing was really moving *out there*? I came to theorize that a change in my consciousness was happening to lead the way for a change in my physical reality.

I regard this as evidence that *belief*, as an aspect of mind, does determine what's possible and impossible in physical reality for an individual. The mental micro-movements hinted that I, with my belief, was changing.

This soon gave way to the second type of micro-movements, which are *physically observable*. These are undoubtable to my eyes. When I've asked Cierra to come and see if she observed the same thing I did, she has concurred. This was no longer just happening inside my head.

We could both see the object trembling and pivoting in almost imperceptible amounts.

The moment your eyes see the same subtle movement, your mind will suddenly perk up. The contrast with utter stillness will be great enough for you to notice. It'll make you look twice. You may not believe your eyes at first, and the effect may subside, but you won't forget what you think you saw.

You'll keep an eye out for it to happen again, since this new experience will pique your curiosity. If your excitement and tension is too great in that moment, though, it might be a while before it happens again.

But if you can remain cool and relaxed, continuing the application of A&I, remembering to relax the body and use the Mind-Stopping Breath, the micro-movements will soon return.

Extending Your Relaxation Toward the Micro-Movements

Along with the instructions given above, this one can help you take advantage of the micro-movement phase. At this point, the object has received almost enough energy to really move. It's trembling with it.

You can boost your influence by directing your sense of bodily relaxation *toward the object*. Take a few deep breaths first, and with each exhalation, feel your muscles soften and relax. This is a soothing, enjoyable sensation. Then, exhale again, this time relaxing *toward* the object, expanding that sense of relaxation *out in front of you*. This might seem like an unusual concept, but it's easy to apply.

Imagine that your sitting next to a friend who is stressed out or sad. She's breathing rapidly and you can see her face is taught with emotion. Her jaw is clenched and her shoulders are raised tightly toward her ears. You're listening to her tell you an experience she just had which has obviously upset her.

Instinctually, you begin breathing more slowly and softening your own muscles as you listen to her. You let your shoulders drop, loosen your neck and unclench your fists.

As you relax yourself this way, you mentally extend your relaxation toward her. As her friend, you want her to start feeling better too.

You *intend your relaxation to make contact* with her. You might not know how to really send the relaxation, but your intention is enough. After a minute or two, you notice her breathing slow down, her shoulders slacken, and her face soften.

You'll want to treat the object the way you treated your friend in the scenario above.

Watching the micro-movements, cultivate that same kind of relaxation in your own body, as well as your mind. If you notice that you've been mentally trying too hard, or have slipped into trying to *think* it into moving, then let that effort go. You'll notice a sense of ease and spaciousness in your mind when you do that. It's an experience of simplicity.

Next, expand that feeling beyond your body, out in front of you. You could simply imagine that the relaxation is so expansive that it extends beyond your skin boundary, like a cloud passing through tiny openings in a membrane. When you do that, the micro-movement will blossom into a fully observable motion.

Time Blurring and Sleep Visions

I want to share a strange thing that happened in my own Level Two development before I succeeded at moving the object.

While applying my A&I, I would periodically imagine what it would look like if the object actually began turning. I would simply pretend. I wondered if doing this might somehow affect the present reality and cause a change.

I wouldn't imagine anything extreme like the object spinning wildly or flying off the needle. Just a nudge or slight turn. While my eyes perceived only stillness, I visualized the future motion of the object in my mind's eye. Then I would overlay the imagined scene onto the object in the present moment. I call this "time blurring."[*]

Once in a while as I drifted off to sleep at night, this future-based image of the moving object would spontaneously appear again in my mind's eye. Behind my closed lids I would watch the imaginary object turning steadily on the needle. It was similar to watching a memory, but with an added element. I could feel an almost physical sensation in my mind. It was as if I felt the actual motion of the object *from within*.

This spontaneous image would only last a few moments, a minute at most, and then I would continue on to the darkness of sleep. This is called "sleep shifting."

---

[*] I don't list *time blurring* as a technique in the method taught here because I'm not sure if it did have an effect on the object or not. However, I mention it here as a possibility that it was, and at the least as a proposal for further experimentation by the reader.

Level Two

I believe the sleep shifting was a sign that I was finally changing my default model of reality. My subconscious mind was beginning to accept that I could actually move an object without touching it and without the interference of heat, wind or anything else. My inner non-believer was getting tired of resisting, and my inner skeptic was prepared to collect new and unexpected data.

One evening, in the middle of the usual, no-motion training session, the object swung in a slow arc around the needle. It was just as it looked in pre-sleep visions.

Finally, success!

15. Troubleshooting

If, after you reach the stage of micro-movements, you remain stuck there for a few sessions, it will be fair to suspect there could be obstacles present which have nothing to do with your work.

One common obstacle is that over time, the tip of the needle has burrowed into the surface of the tinfoil or paper. The burrowing could have occurred during the micro-movements, or just by sitting on the needle and letting time do the rest. It's nearly impossible to see the tiny indentation with the naked eye.

The telekinetic force we're cultivating at these levels is simply too weak to prevail over the slightest friction. As you practice more and more, your ability will get stronger. But in the beginning, even the least resistance will be enough to confound you.

Luckily the solution is simple. Just reset the object on the needle. If you're worried that the needle will find its way into the existing burrow, then throw it away and use a new piece of tinfoil or paper.

Another obstacle has to do with energy. By having your physical hands in the vicinity of the object, they help to extend your body's energy field toward it. Your left hand will have a greater effect on the left side of the object while the same applies to the right hand and the right side.

If all other forces remain equal, then you may be *accidentally holding the object in stasis*. Even though the object and the environment are in contact with your energy, if the field is in a state of balance, then the object stays put where it is.

If you suspect this is the case, slowly pull your hands away from the glass, then replace them at a different angle to the object. For instance, move your left hand forward (further away from you) and pull your right hand back (closer to you). Relax your body and mind as if you were starting a new session, and continue applying your A&I. You may notice a new response from the object within a few moments.

The shift in hand position in relation to the object's angle can create enough energetic dissonance or imbalance to influence the object unequally. This unbalanced stimulation then causes it to move.

The image on the next page shows the object "balanced" between the two equally positioned hands.

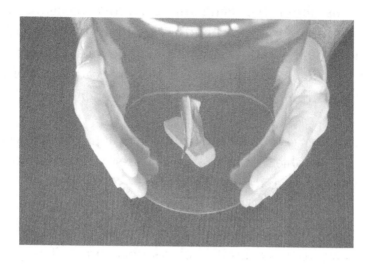

The image below shows how to adjust the hands to *unbalance* their influence on the object. Notice the hand on the left is pulled back closer to the body, and closer to that half of the object. The hand on the right is farther away from the body, and closer to the opposite half of the object.

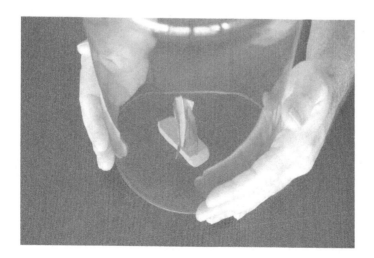

Troubleshooting

Be cautious about overusing this corrective measure. You should avoid moving your hands every time you hit a period of stillness, which in the beginning will be most of the time. Every time you move your hands in hopes of causing an effect you risk disturbing your A&I and the flow of energy.

Be patient after you make the hand correction, give it several minutes. The object might still require more time to be affected by the altered flow of energy.

To watch the hand placement correction being done, go to: http://www.defyyourlimitsbook.com/beta.html. It is part of the video on Control, the third video on that page.

Another thing to remember is to keep your hands relaxed at all times. Do the hands below look relaxed or tense?

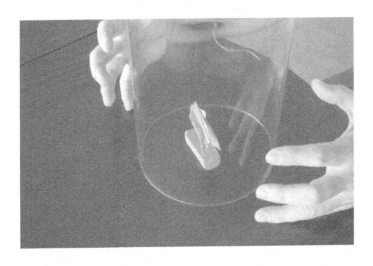

Obviously, they're tense, and they're revealing that the mind is also tense. You will note relaxed posture of the hands in the other photos throughout the book, and in the videos.

As in Level One, you can be confident that you have succeeded with Level Two when you can exhibit some control over the speed and direction of the object.

Since you are using a glass barrier, the doubt that this could be the effect air movement will diminish greatly. Yet because your hands are touching the glass, you might wonder if your hands are heating it, and therefore heating the air inside the container. This would cause convection, the movement of air caused by a cycle of heating and cooling. You might suspect that the convection is causing the object to behave like a ship's sail, moving against the force of the air current.

This is the reason for developing your telekinesis to the point where you can change the direction and speed of the object. Simple air convection can't do that, but your intention, relaxation, and application of the breathing technique can.

For example, with practice you'll be able to make the object turn in one direction during a long inhalation, then to reverse the spin during the next exhalation. You'll also be able to pause the movement while holding the breath at the top of the inhale. This shows that *you* are the controlling agent, not the presumed convection.

If the convection theory still bothers you, don't worry. We'll dismantle it with Level Three.

Troubleshooting

For an example of successful Level Two movement, visit http://www.defyyourlimitsbook.com/gamma.html

One you have succeeded with Level Two, then continue on to Level Three.

16. Mental Models and Basic Principles

In the beginning of the book I wrote that I felt directionless in my attempts to do telekinesis. As I continued my journey of trial and error, certain ideas became clear and stood out for their helpfulness. By sharing these ideas with you before you go further in your training, you will find your way to success much more easily. More importantly, you will be able to weather the inevitably long periods of stillness with patient confidence. This is especially important with Levels Three and Four. You have already been introduced to some of these, and I repeat them here because of their importance.

Also, taking these ideas into consideration ahead of time will reduce the noise in your head that will arise during a telekinesis training session.

Curiosity, philosophizing, and critical thinking are natural motions of the mind. They are necessary to our day to day activities. However, for our purposes it will be necessary to *decrease that noise*. Doing so will boost the force of your mental intention. The following ideas will answer future questions now, which is preferable to you turning those questions over in your mind during a session while you're trying to move the object.

110

We could categorize the ideas below as *mental models*. They help to define the territory that we're entering, and to set up rules of engagement. We need to be clear that these models are intended as theories to be explored and tested by their effects, and *should not be confused with facts*.

Some of these theories will seem to accord very closely with how we experience telekinesis and other phenomena. They will seem reliable. Because of that, we could also regard these models as working hypotheses. A hypothesis is a proposed explanation for why something happens the way it does. It is unproven, but functions as a starting point to experiment with and to get closer to explaining what's really going on.

Our inner skeptic knows to not become attached to our working hypotheses. They are merely helpful tools. Once we find a better tool, we can discard the old one. This entire training method is a working hypothesis. It produces results, but future discoveries will surpass it. The ideas below are not meant to become dogma. They are a map, not the destination.

Energy Follows Attention

This is the most important principle in this telekinesis training method, *energy follows attention*. Memorize those three words and think of them often. This is an ancient idea found in meditative traditions across the planet. I learned it in my study and practice of Tibetan Buddhism*. In that tradition, feeling the subtle qualities of the interior body, then drawing energy to specific areas of it are key practices. Similar

---

* Also known as Vajrayana Buddhism.

concepts are found in Tai Chi, Chi Kung and the Indian Yoga tradition, among others.

There are commonly known phrases that reflect this understanding. For example, "What you resist, persists" and "What you focus on, expands." While meditators use this understanding to affect their bodies and minds, others use it to affect their careers, their relationships, and their connection with spirit.

When people, particularly young people who've watched a lot of science fiction movies, are introduced to telekinesis, many of them assume that they are supposed to somehow force energy out of their hands or out of their bodies and shoot it at the object.

This approach is putting the cart before the horse. Our method is much more simple. You simply need to place your attention on the object you'd like to affect. If the appropriate conditions of body and mind are present, the energy will naturally and effortlessly move to that object in its own way.

Tension, Relaxation, and the Flow of Energy

Imagine a garden hose. When you bend it enough, it prevents the water from flowing through it, and pressure accumulates. When you release it, the bend disappears and the water flows freely through the rest of the hose, dissipating the pressure. This describes the relationship between your mind, body, and energy.

If your mind is filled with stress, pressure, and judgement, or if it's distracted, multi-tasked, or racing with thoughts, it's in

112

a state of tension. This prevents the flow of energy. Because a person's state of mind is mirrored in his or her body, if the mind is tense, then the body will be tense as well. If the body is tense, then that prevents the flow of energy.

During your training sessions, you will need to cultivate both a relaxed mind and body. Fortunately, it's easier than some would assume. The beauty of the body and mind is that they are in relationship to each other. Instead of trying to relax a tense mind by working on the mind, you would direct your intention to relaxing the body.

Do you notice how people breathe when they're angry, upset, or scared? You'll see their shoulders rising up and down, and in some you'll also notice their necks straining with every breath. Meanwhile their stomachs are frozen, unmoving. Now think of how babies breathe while they're safely and happily sleeping in their cribs.

Their tummies resemble little balloons, inflating and deflating with every inhale and exhale. Experienced meditators breathe the same way while in their seated meditation posture. This is how most people breath when they're deeply relaxed and content.

Meditators know that if they want to relax their minds, they can do so by first relaxing the body. *To relax the body, they breathe in a relaxing way.* This is why we use the Mind-Stopping Breath technique. It promotes the flow of energy toward anything you place your attention on. In our case, we place it on the object.

Energy – What Are We Referring To?

Let's review some basic facts about the human body, facts that even children are aware of. The body has various networks running through it which accomplish different tasks. We have our cardiovascular system, comprised of the heart and the circulatory system. This system is so obvious that we can see the veins under our own skin.

We also have a nervous system, which includes the brain, the spinal cord, and the network of nerves that spread throughout the body. There are different kinds of nerves, performing different functions. Some stimulate muscles, others transmit pain. Others tell the brain where our body and limbs are positioned in the surrounding space.

Information is sent along this system through the use of electricity and chemical structures like hormones. The long strands of nerve tissue in the spinal cord can be easily seen, for instance during spinal surgery. Yet the nervous structures and connections inside the brain itself are far more difficult to discern without the assistance of microscopes and scanning technologies.

We now know that the heart and brain both emit electromagnetic fields. Other producers of electromagnetic fields include our planet, thunderstorms, your microwave, the sun, and every electrical outlet in your house. They're everywhere. For the most part, they are measureable with technology, but invisible to the naked eye.

We should remain open to the possibility that there are other types of electromagnetic fields that we haven't learned to measure with instruments yet. Like electromagnetic fields, the subtle energy system of the body is also invisible to the naked eye. Some people claim to see it, and this is what has generally been referred to as the "aura."

Highly refined systems such as Chinese medicine and acupuncture have mapped out how this subtle energy flows through the body, similarly to the cardiovascular and nervous systems. These modalities have been in development for thousands of years.

Anyone who doesn't believe in subtle energy is probably unaware of its use in other parts of the world. In the early and mid 1900's, the Chinese government promoted the widespread use of acupuncture because of its efficacy and its affordability in treating many types of illness. They built hospitals and research facilities specifically to employ and further develop this healing modality. Today, acupuncture has spread across the world.

The Chinese word for energy is "chi". The Sanskrit word for it is "prana." Both of these terms have entered into normal use outside of Asia, accompanying the spread of martial arts and yoga. One way or another, subtle energy has been a very real part of life for thousands of generations across the planet. It's not some unproven New Age belief, as some still think.

The topics of exactly how subtle energy flows through the body, the various types of energy and their relationship to our greater consciousness are beyond the scope of this book. There are various theories of what this energy actually is, but there still is no generally accepted consensus. Regardless, those who have learned to use it and those who have experienced its healing power all agree that it's real, and it works.

I won't rely on exotic language for this telekinesis training method, so I refer to the phenomena of chi and prana by the English word "energy." Electricity and heat are also forms of energy, as indeed everything we call "matter" is composed of energy. When I use the word energy however, I am not referring to those other types, only to the *subtle force that flows inside our bodies and all around us.*

The earlier exercise *Energy Follows Attention* has already given you a direct experience of feeling the energy in your body.

Invisible Mechanism, Observable Effect

When you use your cell phone, or when you stream a movie onto your laptop via wireless connection, can you see the signal? No, of course you can't. But you know with full confidence that if conditions are right, like having a charged battery, and if you take the proper action, like pushing the correct buttons, that you will achieve the desired effect, the transfer of information.

It is the same with telekinesis. For all four levels, your task is to create the right conditions, such as relaxing your body and quieting the mind, and to take proper action, such as directing your attention and intention toward the object. During the many hours I have spent practicing telekinesis, I have *never* felt a physical connection between my body and the object. Even though I have felt a variety of sensations *inside* parts of my body, no reliable pattern energy felt outside my body has emerged.

Mental Models and Basic Principles

In this type of telekinesis, you do the technique, but you can't see or feel anything reaching out across space and touch the object. You can only wait, applying the mental and physical instructions, until the object moves.

When you become proficient at the breathing technique, you will be able to affect the direction and speed of the object, which will give you more confidence in the telekinetic effect. At that level, though, you still will not feel any kind of physical link with the object. This can be a difficult concept for some to accept.

It's like going fishing in a strange parallel universe where some of the rules have changed. You have your pole, and there's a fish in the water. Yet you have no fishing line. You simply sit there working with your mind according to the instructions. The fishing pole is like your body. When your mind and your pole are just right, a fish will jump out of the water and land at your feet – no fishing line involved.

Lest the fishing analogy strikes you as unreasonable, remember that you go through a similar process every time you make a phone call, watch TV, open a garage door, have an X-Ray, send a text, wave your hand in front of a paper towel dispenser, and so on. Something *is* being transmitted, you just can't feel the transmission itself.

Interconnectedness

Telekinesis is neither miracle nor magic. There is a mechanism behind it which is still largely unknown. Even though people know how to actualize the telekinetic effect, and we theorize the involvement of subtle energy, we don't know all the intricate details of what happens.

If someone calls it a miracle, it is only because they don't understand it. For our purposes, we can assume that it has its place in our universe, this place where everything in it derives its identity from its relationship to everything else. We are all interconnected on many levels.

If you could shrink yourself to the size of a skin cell, you would witness a constant exchange of chemical compounds and microbes entering and leaving the body, transported by air, temperature, and moisture.

When you are in conversation with someone, *who you are changes* as you gain new and different information from that person. Some of that information is verbal. You also subconsciously receive and transmit information through physical cues, how you hold and move your body. We also gain information about other people and our world through our sense of smell, taste, hearing, and touch.

Many people are aware that they can gain information intuitively, in ways that don't depend on the five physical senses. A mother can just know that something is wrong with her child, either one room, one mile, or one country away. People can have dreams that hint at or directly show an event yet to come into their lives.

Mental Models and Basic Principles

The sun's electromagnetic field affects that of the earth, and the effect ripples into our atmosphere, reaching all the way into our bodies.

It will be useful for you to contemplate the various ways that we share connections and affect each other. Think of it as the transmission of information. Science has already shown that physical matter is mostly composed of empty space. Even what we used to regard as subatomic particles, when looked at more closely, resemble *brief events* more than they do *things*.

As you continue your telekinesis training, consider that you may simply be sending information across a short distance, altering the behavior of the object. An even more provocative hypothesis would be that you're affecting the information in your *entire* environment.

It's almost as if you're re-programming your experience of the object and its relationship to the table it's resting on, its relationship to the room you're in, and especially its relationship to you. This idea may not bring us much closer to proving how telekinesis works, but it will help to pull telekinesis out of the realm of hocus pocus and abracadabra.

How Physical Perception Separates Us from Reality

There are neuroscientists today who say that the brain operates as a filter, or an input reducer. It receives information via the physical senses, then sorts, labels, and organizes that data, finally delivering a greatly reduced package of experience to our waking consciousness.

Much of the leftover information is kept elsewhere, what some call our subconscious mind. We know that what we receive through our eyes, ears, nose, tongue, and skin isn't everything there is out there.

If a tree falls in the forest and there's no one there to hear it, does it still make a sound?

The answer is "no", because sound is something that requires an eardrum and a brain in order to manifest in one's experience. When a tree falls, waves are sent through the air. If someone is in the area, those waves will enter the ears. They will stimulate these organs to transmit information to the brain through the nervous system, which will then convert it into what you call "sound".

If a brain and eardrum are absent, so is *sound*.

It's the same with your eyes. Color doesn't exist *out there*, it's something your brain produces for you when particular wavelengths enter the organ of your eye, sending information through the optical nerve to the brain. The actual process is far more complex than that, but I'm sure you understand the point.

Mental Models and Basic Principles

We can only see a limited section of the full electromagnetic spectrum. If the frequency of the waves is outside those limits, our eyes don't perceive them.

There is so much happening inside and outside of us that we just can't perceive. When you look out at your world, all you're really seeing is a translation of those few signals which our physical organs are capable of registering.

What you see, hear, taste, touch and smell is not that different from what the screen on your cell phone presents you with. The real world *out there* is composed of innumerable wavelengths and brief events in space, all transmitting more information than our human personality can handle in one moment.

Wouldn't you agree that the more we learn about reality, the less impossible phenomena like telekinesis seem to be?

Our Minds Are Not Entirely Our Own

Language is a significant factor in how our brain filters and sorts our experience. Because we learned language from our parents, we automatically absorbed their points of view on religion, politics, interpersonal relationships, history, ethics. We also absorbed their beliefs about what is, and isn't, *real*. This is why the beliefs and attitudes of our species change so slowly.

A novel thought is a rare thing. When we think, we usually recycle ideas adopted from other people. Along with that, we choose our communities by how much our inherited thoughts match those of other group members. This is how we, as adults, seek out religious groups, social circles, and careers.

In a strange way, then, if you're the black sheep in the family who is interested in the paranormal, metaphysics, or non-religious spirituality, some part of your psyche may feel threatened, even if most of you is on board with this material. Deep down inside, we fear rejection by our communities. It's a survival instinct, because being part of a community has always been the best guarantor of a long life.

You are an intelligent being capable of free will. When you hear the contradictory opinions and proclamations of your parents, teachers and friends in the back of your mind, disguised as your own thoughts, know that they are not.

Telekinesis, like other psi phenomena, is your opportunity to see and do things that aren't even possible *in other people's version* of reality. Telekinesis is a special way for you to obtain unique information about the world. This will help you

Mental Models and Basic Principles

become your own person, with your own ideas, rather than remaining a duplicate of someone else's social programming.

This is possible not because of the telekinesis itself, but because this training is a vehicle for learning to be open to the unknown.

We Have Two Minds

We are still establishing mental models here, ideas which provide a framework that we can operate from. The mind is defined, dissected, and analyzed in many ways by neuroscience, psychology, transpersonal psychology, parapsychology, physics, metaphysics, religion, and spirituality. For the purpose of telekinesis training, we will regard the mind in yet a different way.

Let us divide the mind into two types. One is the *conceptual mind*, the thinking mind. We experience this when we're speaking with someone, writing an email message, forming opinions, engaging in problem solving, and when we're daydreaming.

The other type is the *nonconceptual mind*, the one which operates without words and without logical structure. Compared to the conceptual mind, we could say this is the silent mind. We experience it especially during meditation, on the boundary of being asleep and awake, and in moments of grace and awe. Let's establish that the mental factors of *attention* and *intention* live here, in the silent mind.

Both types are usually simultaneously present throughout our waking experience. They work together to produce our experience of being conscious and alive in these bodies. For example, you may be with a friend when a craving for coffee arises in your mind. Your thinking mind structures the words, which you say aloud to your friend, "Want to go get a cup of coffee?"

Just before uttering those words, and after the craving arose, you *decided* to invite your friend to coffee. Before your mouth, tongue, and vocal chords began producing language, there arose the silent, invisible intention to speak. It was an ultra-fast event in your mind. It came and went without you ever noticing it.

During each Level Three and Four training session, you will practice isolating and prolonging that usually brief experience of intention. You'll see that the noisy thinking mind can rob your intention of potency.

Let's return to the idiom of the boiling pot. It's an image which applies to both intention and attention. Visualize yourself standing at your kitchen stove, and the pot of water is resting on a burner. Your goal is to boil the water. When your attention and intention are in effect, the pot remains on the burner, absorbing the necessary heat to boil the water.

Yet every time you get distracted, or your mind gets flooded with thoughts and emotions, you lift the pot off the burner. When that happens, it loses the accumulated heat and it's not until your mind settles and re-establishes a steady attention and intention that you set the pot back on the burner. Our two minds, left unmanaged, work against each other during telekinesis.

Keep in mind that this isn't a "right or wrong" type of activity. It's something that comes naturally over time. The more time you spend in training, the more familiar you'll become with these subtle aspects of mind at an experiential level. Over time, your intention and attention will become steady enough to actualize the telekinetic effect.

Energy Accumulates Over Time

In this style of telekinesis, it's important to regard it as *the accumulation of energy over a period of time*. Telekinesis is not like sending a projectile across space and immediately causing movement upon impact. Rather, it's like charging your cell phone.

The recharge is not an instant process. You need to leave it plugged in for a period of time before the battery absorbs the requisite amount of energy. At that point it will vibrate, ring, and display images for you.

Remembering this when working with the object will help you to be patient. You will understand that while it appears that nothing is happening, *something crucial is happening*, albeit invisibly. Take the attitude that every time you sit with the object and direct your attention and intention toward it, you're charging that battery.

Your energy is imperceptibly heading toward the object over a period of time. At a certain point, without warning, you'll discover that it's charged enough because that is when the object will start to move.

This effect happens much quicker at Level Three than at Level Four. Each succeeding level will require more time than the preceding one. You already experienced this when going from Level One to Level Two.

You will notice a strange effect which relates to the analogy of the charged battery. This is something that you will experience after having been successful with at least Level

Two for some time. Imagine now that you sit before your object as it rests inside the glass container. Your hands are in position, and after directing your A&I to the object for some time while using the breathing technique, the object begins to spin.

You continue producing the effect for a few minutes. Then it's time to rest or go do something else. However, after you take your hands away and stop applying your mind toward it, *it continues to turn*.

It even continues to turn for many seconds or even a couple minutes. It behaves as if it's dissipating the accumulated energy, but I can't say for certain if that's what's happening. This can occur at any level, especially Level Four.

This is just one example of the sometimes illogical, spontaneous, and contradictory nature of the telekinetic effect. Sometimes with this stuff all we can say is, "I don't know what's happening, but it's happening."

We'll discuss even stranger effects in the following pages.

Anomalies of Relationship

You will notice that once you have become proficient at Level Two and Three, it takes about the same amount of time for movement to begin – as long as you have been using the same piece of tin foil or paper for a long period of time.

This may sound strange, but you are establishing a relationship, a link, with the object during your training. Aside from the evidence by way of its reaction to your attention and intention, I don't know of any other way to show you that you are in relationship with it.

However, there is an anomaly I should mention here, which you will undoubtedly notice yourself assuming that you are training on a regular basis.

This is something that will occur only after already having succeeded at moving the object. I noticed this a few weeks after my first movement. Sometimes, immediately upon walking into the room where the training area was set up, the object would begin to turn. It's as if it already knew what I wanted to do with it, and began responding right away, *even before I sat down in front of it.*

There are variations of this anomaly. Sometimes, it was when I sat down in front of it and *merely glanced at it* that it would begin to turn.

In experiments with two separate objects, each in their own glass container, I would direct my attention to one, but out of distraction I would briefly glance at the other, and *it* would move instead of the originally intended object.

I refer to this effect as "sticky energy," though I am inconclusive as to what is really happening here. I suspect that in the case of having two objects close to each other, the one I have spent more time with may be receiving the energy, thus "taking it away" from the other, even though I want the energy to go to the other.

In neuroscience, there's the phrase, "Cells that fire together, wire together." This expresses the fact that weak bonds between neurons will strengthen through repeated stimulation, increasing their efficiency. Perhaps something similar is happening here which allows one object to respond to the energy intended for another nearby.

17. The Catch & The Lookaway

There are two more "eye effects" I'd like to share before you continue to Level Three. They are both extremely subtle and can make the difference between micro-movements and complete motion at Levels Three and Four. Like everything else I'm introducing here, these are phenomena I discovered during my own development.

The Catch

Imagine sitting before the glass container now, and you've been applying yourself for thirty minutes without any signs of movement. Your body and mind have finally relaxed, and the noise in your head is no longer distracting you. Your A&I are steady.

Then suddenly your eyes perceive actual movement. But a split second later, your *conceptual* mind realizes what it's seeing. Then the object stops. It only had time to move half a millimeter before freezing in place. Now you're perplexed and frustrated. It *felt* like it was going to keep moving, why did it stop?

In that split second of movement, your heart pulsed a little quicker while a storm of thoughts and emotions erupted in your mind. Perhaps that's what stopped it – the excitement caused bodily tension which immediately blocked the flow of energy, or broke the fragile connection.

Or was it something else?

Until the thinking mind picked up on the fact that you were influencing something from a distance, the rest of your overall being was perfectly fine with it. Your eyes let the scene enter, and your body seemed fine as well. No part of you was particularly responsive to the movement until your personality, your *ego,* caught up to what was happening.

When I have those moments, it feels as if my eyes stop their transmission of A&I and instead, *freeze* the object. That's why I call this effect *The Catch.* The moving object got caught up in my *ordinary expectation* of reality, and my ego mind put a stop to the effect right then and there.

There is a deeply etched belief inside most of us that telekinesis is impossible, a fantasy. Could our ego be affecting reality as well, to *prevent breaking any rules*? Science has produced evidence that this could be the case.

Charles Tart, Ph.D. discusses "psi missing" in *The End of Materialism*. He discusses this concept in the context of psi experiments using both believers and non-believers as test subjects.

In these experiments, the believers scored significantly above chance expectations, which indicated that they had some type

---

* See References

of telepathic ability. How do you think the non-believers scored?

They would have been happy with an absence of positive hits, indicating no special influence or ability was taking place at all. This would prove their disbelief to be correct. But something else happened.

Instead, they scored *extra* badly. Their results were the inverse of the believers', also exceeding chance expectations, but in the opposite direction. They had inadvertently used their telepathic ability to influence their results.

This not only shows that anyone can have a psychic influence, but that they can do so without being consciously aware of it.

When I *feel* my eyes catching the object's movement and stopping it, it seems that a part of me is trying to put the brakes on. It's my inner non-believer. Ironically, it's using telekinesis, something it doesn't believe in, to stop the movement.

This is an important consideration when showing telekinesis to a group of people, especially people who are doubtful of or even aggressive toward the notion of psi abilities. You might find yourself unable to do publicly what had become easy for you at home when you're by yourself.

One of those observers might be *catching* the object and holding it still with their own mind. They won't consciously know that this is what they're doing of course, because it's their subconscious belief that is producing the effect and ruining your efforts. I have no doubt that several non-believers can unknowingly work in tandem to make sure nothing moves.

The Lookaway

The Lookaway was a phenomenon I accidentally produced during my own training. Eventually I used it to create a solution to *the Catch*.

Similar to the *Refrigerator*, the *Lookaway* is a method of distracting the mind and getting it out of the way so that the attention, intention, and energy can reach out and contact the object without any interference.

There were many times when after long periods of non-movement, I would carelessly look away from it and let my mind ponder other things while my hands and body stayed in place. Only then, in that moment of moving my eyes away from the object, would it begin to move.

I realized that mentally *letting go* is as important a concept in telekinesis as it is in conventional styles of meditation.

This effect also happened in those moments when I decided to take a break or quit for the day. In that moment of letting go, I released my expectations, hopes, and impatience. Simultaneous with that moment of release, my energy was freed to reach out and connect with the object, finally producing the sought-after movement.

I must admit, there's an unnerving realization that the ego can't really participate fully in telekinesis. It has *its* rules, and our deeper nature has its own. Fortunately, that's exactly why we can use the *Lookaway* to resolve the *Catch*.

When you notice the object getting caught by your mind, just look away. Think of something else for a couple of seconds. Also, check your body for tension. Take a nice deep breath and let yourself melt as you forget about the whole project. Relax.

Wait a few moments, then look again. You might notice that it's begun to turn. If it hasn't yet, let your mind remain extremely soft while you gently engage the Mind-Stopping-Breath, just for one or two cycles. If necessary, re-adjust your hands. Then, *let go*.

18. Recipe for Success

Motivation is only one of several qualities you'll need to progress all the way through Level Four. If you've clarified your motivation for learning telekinesis, that'll serve as the foundation for the other desirable qualities, which I'll describe below.

My Bachelor's degree was in computer science, which required a minor in mathematics. I really dislike math. It doesn't come naturally to me. My brain ached as I tried to understand the concepts, and I was regularly filled with anxiety whenever an exam was scheduled. My middle-of-the-road grades reflected that.

In my senior year, I took two semesters of astronomy in order to fulfill the science requirement to graduate. I fell in love with it. It showed me the beauty and perfection of the cosmos. It also involved a lot of math. Interestingly, I didn't mind. I even liked it, and I willingly worked harder at it than I did for my other math classes. I was no longer driven by a sense of requirement.

I had become *passionate* about astronomy. The passion drove me to understand the material because I loved the topic, so I willingly pursued my studies, working harder than I normally would to absorb the material.

The more passionate you feel about this work, the more persistent you will be with the training. This is important because for many people, telekinesis takes time. It took me somewhere around eight weeks to accomplish Level Two. That was at least forty hours of sitting in front of the object trying to make it move, and seeing nothing but absolute stillness. Does that sound obsessive? It's not, it's being persistent.

In the internet age, instant gratification has removed opportunities for people to develop persistence. Your persistence will grow naturally as long as you have the passion to see this through. The same goes for patience. If you are not a patient person, you will either give up quickly or your patience will grow through the course of accomplishing this training.

Persistent people are usually self-driven. This is important. After spending years watching my meditation students develop in their own way, I can say that it's the ones who were self-driven who made the most discoveries and who reaped the greatest benefits from their meditation practice. The same will be true with you.

Integrity may seem like an unexpected quality for telekinesis, but we must acknowledge that people have a funny way of fooling themselves. We need to be more like scientists and less like magicians with this work, and to be honest with what we're doing.

For example, at Level One, there isn't a glass barrier between you and the object. The instructions state that your hands need to remain motionless, and distant enough from the object to minimize the effect of warm air moving the object.

At the end of your second or third session, when nothing had happened yet, strange little thoughts might have cropped up such as "Well, maybe I need to move my hands just a little to get the energy going." Then the object will have wiggled and moved a little bit, and you may have been tempted to conclude that it really was some energy moving the object. You might have been ready to celebrate telekinetic success, but you didn't because you could admit that you were just moving the air.

I will make it easy for you to stay in your integrity as you follow the training, because all you have to do is follow the instructions. If you deviate from the instructions, make sure your radar is set on high alert for self-deception.

The instructions do leave enough room for creativity, don't worry. You need your creativity and problem solving skills for a couple of reasons. First, there might be limitless ways to learn and actualize telekinesis. What I'm teaching you here is my way, the way I learned based on my past experience. I don't know everything, obviously. Since I'm passing everything I know on to you, you will learn faster than I did, which will give you more time to see new possibilities and consider other methods.

Second, I'm guiding you into your internal space. This includes your mental processes, and how your physical body feels. I'm using words to describe what I *think* is happening inside of you, but the fact is that you might use different words for the same experience. I may give an instruction that only partly describes an aspect of your mind, but for you to know what I'm talking about, you need to feel around inside of yourself to find that aspect.

How would you describe the color blue to someone who can't see? This isn't that extreme, but it touches on why you need to be broad minded when working with these instructions.

Do you care what other people think about you? Of course, we all do. Research shows that most of us make decisions based on environmental cues, including how you think people will react to you. When you go to a bookstore, do you feel a little uncomfortable when someone else sees what section you're browsing? When you buy personal products at the grocery store, are you hyper aware of who's standing in line next to you, or who the cashier is?

We all do that, and I think it's because we know in our bones that our survival is a group effort. Not too long ago, if you were cast out of your community, it meant shame, loneliness, starvation and eventual death. That risk of rejection from our personal communities drives us all the time, even when we're all alone in a room.

We're all members of several communities. For example, you have your spouse or family, your coworkers, your religious group. We're even vigilant of people's opinions of us at the gym or salon.

If words like "rebel," "marches to the beat of his or her own drum," "introvert," "artist," or "independent" have ever been used to describe you, then you have little to concern yourself with in this arena. However, if you derive your identity from being "dependable," "always was a good boy/girl," or if you work in a role that depends on maintaining a status quo and not rocking the boat, then listen to the following advice.

Don't tell anyone what you're doing. Do not say one word because the look on someone's face when you tell them you are trying to learn how to move something with your mind could be enough to shame you into stopping.

People tend to ridicule and bully individuals who challenge their beliefs about the world. At the next office holiday party, the target for teasing could be you, the weirdo who believes mind over matter is real. That advice may irritate you because part of you sees the light in this work, and you want to add even more light to our world.

If that's the case with you, I recommend you follow through with your training then, and become capable at repeating the effect at all four levels. Then, don't just tell people, *show* them. You might also remind them that we have these things called cell phones, satellites, and microwaves, which they *believe in* yet probably have no idea how they actually work.

19. Level Three*

The difference between Level Two and Level Three is the position of the hands. All else remains the same. Instead of touching the glass with your hands, space them about a thumb's length from the sides.

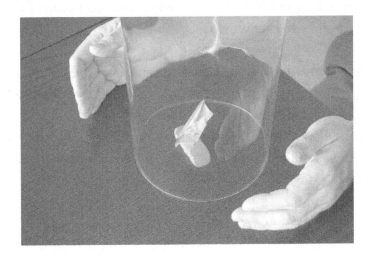

Because of the lack of hand contact with the glass, Level Three is like taking the training wheels off a bicycle. The child might be afraid that they were the only things keeping her from falling down, and she may doubt her ability to ride. Soon

---

* Estimated time for success: one to three months.

enough, her confidence takes over and she develops her balance well enough to ride freely, without fear of tipping over.

With enough practice, you'll have as much success in Level Three as in Level Two. Don't be discouraged if your first successful movement in Level Three takes more time than Level Two did. All you have to do is continue a regular course of training sessions, using the techniques you've learned so far, and you'll be successful. Persistence wins the day at Level Three, so ignore that voice of impatience that's bound to show up.

Why would Level Three take longer than Level Two? Not only does your energy need to negotiate the glass barrier as it did with Level Two, but now it originates further away from the object, assuming that your hands help extend your energy field. Or maybe we just *believe* that the glass makes it more difficult. That's why it's important to ignore it as much as possible.

Keep your eyes open for micro-movements, and use the same troubleshooting techniques you used before.

After your first success, repeat the experiment with the hands a thumb's length away from the glass until you feel confident that you can actualize the effect with good regularity. This doesn't mean that you get to a point where it begins moving as soon as you intend it, but rather that every time you try, after a sufficient period of settling in and of energy accumulation by the object, it begins to move.

Level Three

For example, let's say after several successes you notice that it takes about five minutes before the object starts to move. You know that during the first five minutes you can apply the breathing technique, relax your body and mind, and steadily apply your A&I to the object. You know that around the five-minute mark, you can expect to see movement.

Once you have established a level of confidence similar to the above example, it's time to stretch your ability by moving your hands farther away. You might try an extra half-thumb's length from the glass. Just move your hands far enough away so you no longer have an effect on the object. Then make that your new starting point.

Every time you put more distance between your hands and the object, take the same attitude you had when you were a complete beginner. Let go of any expectations, and of any impatience, and simply apply the technique with a sense of innocence. Be open to taking *as long as necessary* before the effect occurs again.

When you find success at the new distance, spend several sessions there gaining proficiency with control and speed, just as you did at earlier levels.

When you can still actualize telekinesis while keeping the hands a palm's width away from the glass, you'll be ready to move on to Level Four.

To watch a video of Level Three telekinesis, please visit: http://www.defyyourlimitsbook.com/delta.htm

---

20. Introduction to Level Four Training

I see that little girl on her new bicycle, coming down the street. She smiles and waves as she passes, freed from the weight of the training wheels. At the last moment, I see her eyes narrow, and a look of determination comes over her face. She reaches the end of the street, then turns around and starts riding back. Her mother watches from the sidewalk, filled with pride. Excited and a little bit nervous for her baby, her eyes widen as she notices her speeding up. With eyes concentrated on her handle bars, the girl raises her hands, palms out, and zooms up the street. At the last moment, she looks over and hollers, "Look Mom, no hands!"

Welcome to the final stage.

No hands, no proximity to the object. By the end of your training at Level Four, you'll be able to sit several feet away from the object and make it move. It will still be impervious to environmental influences, protected from wind and heat by the glass container, just as it was in Level Three.

Once you have become proficient at Level Four, you will have significantly strengthened and refined the way you use your mind, body, and energy. You'll be able to apply your training to other types of telekinesis, and to other types of psi abilities like remote viewing and Extra Sensory Perception (ESP).

There are other ways of exploring consciousness, such as Lucid Dreaming and the Out of Body Experience (sometimes referred to as Astral Projection), and this training can help with those too. Relaxing the mind and body, applying your intention, and exercising a commitment to regular training are just as important when learning how to experience consciousness beyond the physical body during an OBE.

The social difficulty with Lucid Dreaming and the OBE is that for the most part, these experiences seem to be *subjective* in nature. Most people can't see someone's else's consciousness in a state non-located with the physical body.

In contrast, telekinesis is *objective*. It can absolutely be seen by anyone present in the room, not only the practitioner. That is what gives it the potency to transform not only individuals, but groups. No matter how unbelievable it may seem, it's happening right there in plain sight.

Let's begin now with Level Four training.

Introduction to Level Four Training

21. Level Four, Stage One[*]

At this stage, you should be seated as you were for Levels One, Two, and Three, at the same distance from the edge of the table, the glass container and the object.

Begin each Stage One session as you did in Level Two, by placing your hands on the glass. Spend as much time as necessary to exhibit some control over it. Use everything you've learned, Attention, Intention, Relaxation, and The Mind-Stopping Breath.

Once you've got it moving, distance your hands from the glass, as in Level Three. Maintain your A&I on the object while you make that transition.

If there is a brief loss of connection causing the object to stop, be patient and continue applying your technique. Avoid stressing about it, otherwise it will further weaken the flow of energy.

Check your body and soften any tense areas. Take a few deep breaths and clear your mind of noisy clutter. Begin anew and stay true to the instructions. After a few minutes the

---

[*] Estimated time for success: one to two months.

connection will be re-established and the object will begin moving again.

Continue working in Level Three fashion until you can exhibit a fair amount of influence in terms of speed and direction. This will ensure a good energetic link.

Then, spend some time fully relaxing toward the object and allowing it to move "anyway it wants to" (for lack of a better phrase). Give up any sense of control and place more emphasis on deepening your own relaxation and sharing it with the object. Continue applying your A&I. Think of it this as though you were loading it up with more energy than usual.

After a few minutes, take your hands off the table completely and place them comfortably in your lap. If you've come to subconsciously rely on the use of your hands, this may be a difficult adjustment to make.

It's possible that you developed a belief along the way that an energetic emission from your hands was significantly responsible for the object's movement. If that's the case for you, then this will be a slow process of *dissolving that belief*. I hope the possibility of moving an object just by looking at it excites you enough to want to discard your dependency on the hands.

While transitioning your hands to your lap, continue the rest of the technique. Maintain your overall sense of connection with the object as much as you can. Remember to entrain yourself with the object by noticing its details.

Level Four, Stage One

Notice its colors and creases, remember its odor and taste, and recall how it felt the last time you touched it.

If the connection was maintained when you put your hands in your lap, the object will continue moving. However, if the connection was lost, the object will soon stop.

When it stops, your inner non-believer will rise up and start bellowing "Halleluiah! I knew I was right!" As always, let that doubt have its own corner in the back of your mind while the rest of you gets back to work. Success lies ahead.

Spend at least fifteen minutes applying the technique to the now non-moving object. Avoid becoming impatient, and avoid filling your mind with noise. Remember to use the *Refrigerator* technique when necessary. At this point in your training, it will be easy for you to identify when excess noise has arisen and to instinctively use relaxation to counteract it.

If the object begins to move, continue applying the technique until you feel ready to end the session.

If the object still has not moved, work backwards as a way to end the session. Go back to a Level Three posture, with your hands near, but not touching, the glass. Try to actualize telekinesis at that point.

Then after several minutes, whether or not the object moved, go to Level Two by placing your hands back on the glass. Continue your efforts for several minutes. If by now you haven't moved the object, the most likely reason is that you are tired.

A Note about Exhaustion

You are approaching the most difficult stage of telekinesis taught here. It will be important for you to notice when you've become exhausted.

Athletes can over-train and then find it difficult to recharge. Actors can be overwhelmed and unable to memorize new scripts. Writers can burn themselves out and find it difficult to hold ideas together. Exhaustion is a natural aspect of any type of skill-building.

When this happens, the best thing to do is to *rest*. Exhaustion has a way of provoking feelings of resignation and depression, so you want to rest whenever necessary. Once you've rested, perhaps for two or three days, you can return to your training feeling optimistic and energized. After you've rested, start with Level One to re-establish your confidence, then work your way up from there.

Summarizing Level Four, Stage One

1. Start your session with Level Two, hands on the glass.

2. After a few minutes of motion at Level Two, immediately shift to Level Three, hands off the glass.

3. After a few minutes of Level Three, move your hands to your lap and continue with the rest of the technique.

4. Continue for at least fifteen minutes, regardless of there being movement or not.

5. To end the session, revert to Level Three for a few minutes.

6. Continue backward into Level Two for a few more minutes.

7. End the session when ready.

Train with the Level Four, Stage One sequence until you are able to maintain your connection with the object, and keep it moving, after shifting from Level Three (hands off glass) to Level Four (hands in your lap).

To watch a video of Level Four, Stage One, go to: http://www.defyyourlimitsbook.com/epsilon.html

Once you are able to repeat that level of proficiency with regular success, go to Level Four, Stage 2.

22. Level Four, Stage Two*

First, let's set a fair expectation for success at Stages Two and Three of Level Four. These are likely to require far more time for completion than Levels Two and Three did. Be prepared to spend anywhere from several weeks to months of regular practice before achieving success. Every practitioner is unique, so some will experience results faster than others. Here are the main factors of success at this level:

- Regular practice
- Passion
- Commitment and will
- Staying true to the instructions instead of trying new things out of desperation
- Continually deepening your capacity to relax and to stay present for long periods of time, even after weeks of non-movement with the Level Four portions of the exercises
- Increasing your ability to experience a sense of oneness and connection with the object as described earlier

---

* Estimated time for success: one to three months.

Stage Two is the half-way mark to completion of Level Four. It extends the sequence of training from Stage One, forming a bridge to Stage Three.

Repositioning your table and seating arrangement

You will either add an additional chair to the table now, or be willing to move your chair to the other end of it at the appropriate time in this exercise.

Move the object and its glass container to one end of your table, along with your chair. You will be starting seated close to it as you did in the first three levels.

Repeat the beginning sequence of Stage One, doing Level Two, then Level Three. Then at the moment when you would normally move your hands to your lap, instead *get up and move to the opposite end of the table*. Leave the object where it is.

While you move to the other side, keep your A&I on the object. It's alright if you can't keep your eyes on it while you walk over. It's more important for your mind to remain linked with the object.

Sit down across the table from the object, again with your lands in your lap. The object may still be moving at this point, or it may have stopped. Regardless, continue applying all the techniques you've learned – the relaxation, A&I, the Mind-Stopping Breath, and the rest.

Even if the object remains stopped, continue applying the technique. Remember that energy takes time to build in the object, and in a way, you're completely starting over.

Defy Your Limits   Sean McNamara

Apply the technique for at least twenty minutes regardless of whether or not the object moves, then work backwards as you did in Stage One. Walk back to the other side, sit down, and try again. Then try it using the Level Three technique, then Level Two.

An important note regarding distance. It is still important for you to be able to see the object well enough to entrain with it, so you'll need to adjust the object's position in order to do that. If the object appears blurry from across the table, I suggest you move it in toward the center of the table only as much as necessary for you to be able to see it clearly from both ends.

Level Four, Stage Two

Summarizing Level Four, Stage Two

1. Start your session with Level Two, hands on the glass.

2. After a few minutes of motion at Level Two, immediately shift to Level Three, hands off the glass.

3. After a few minutes of Level Three, stand up slowly and walk to the opposite end of the table. If you can, keep your eyes on the object while you reposition yourself.

4. Sit down gently, keeping your hands in your lap.

5. Continue applying all the techniques from Levels One, Two, and Three (except of course the use of the hands) for at least fifteen minutes, regardless of there being movement or not.

6. To begin closing the session, get up again and sit in your original position.

7. Revert to Level Three for a few minutes.

8. Continue backward into Level Two for a few more minutes.

9. End the session when ready.

Train with the Stage Two sequence until you are able to maintain your connection with the object (and keep it moving) after getting up and moving to the opposite end of the table.

To watch a video of Level Four, Stage Two, go to: http://www.defyyourlimitsbook.com/zeta.html

Further indicators of entrainment at Level Four

If your training regimen is steady, perhaps practicing every day or most days of the week for forty-five minutes to an hour, it is likely that you will experience another indicator of entrainment at this point*.

You probably already experienced the *anomalies of relationship*, mentioned earlier. For example, sometimes when you enter the room or sit down in front of the object, it begins to move even before you've begun applying your A&I.

At Stage Two, you will encounter an extension of the same phenomenon. The object will respond *when you stand up to move to the other side of the table*, and continue moving as you seat yourself and get settled.

If Albert Einstein hadn't already coined the now popular phrase "spooky action at a distance,"** that is exactly how I would refer to this effect. An observer inclined toward the paranormal might see what's happening on the table and suggest that a ghost is making the object move***.

It may even move *more* than when you were actively trying to influence it. This makes sense though, since your thinking

---

* The reader may want to review the section on Entrainment from Level Two.
** This phrase references the topics of entanglement and non-locality, which are much discussed in quantum physics, which is beyond the scope of this book.
*** I must admit that this effect has, at times, led me to wonder if any non-physical or dearly departed beings have an involvement with these experiments.

mind has likely detached itself momentarily to focus on moving your body to another seat. In that moment of distraction, the energy and intention were able to finish what you had begun, without interference from your conceptual mind.

The advantage of this occurrence is that once you've sat down and noticed the movement, you can relax in the confirmation of your connection to the object. This relaxation will extend itself into your re-continued application of A&I, and it will help continue the movement.

You'll become confident that you are in fact still influencing the object, even when it stops during your transition to the other seat.

Let's say a minute or two after moving to the other seat, the object slows down or stops. It is crucial that you remain relaxed and patient. Don't let fear or doubt creep in and cause you to strain your mind. Remember to behave emotionally like a skeptic, not like a believer.

Simply draw in a lung-full of air and hold for a few seconds, then exhale slowly while gently extending your relaxation out to the object. If necessary, repeat this step several times, remaining peaceful throughout. It will eventually respond, verifying your connection.

Once you're able to repeat that level of proficiency with regular success, move on to Stage Three of Level Four.

23. Level Four, Stage Three (Final Stage)[*]

You are now at the final stage, which is extraordinarily simple to describe. Here, the object and glass container are positioned as in Stage Two, on one end of the table. Begin by sitting down at the opposite end of the table, at least three or four feet away.

Apply everything you have already learned: the A&I, the Mind-Stopping Breath, keeping your body and mind relaxed, and expanding your sense of relaxation forward toward the object.

Keep this formula in mind:

$$T + R + I + A = M.$$

Time in Relaxation, Intention, and Attention produce Movement. A lack of any one of the causative factors will have a diminishing effect on how soon movement begins, as well as its speed.

The most important principle to keep in mind at this stage is that *energy accumulates in the object over time*, which you've already learned. Patience is crucial at Stage Three. Without it, you will default to straining with your mental energy, trying

---

[*] Estimated time for success: one to three months

to force a reaction in the object. By now, you know that doesn't work.

If you have stayed true to the instructions beginning with Level One, you will naturally be vigilant against straining and make any necessary correction as soon as it arises. However, we must acknowledge that every new experience can cause us to revert to old patterns.

Stage Three is the most daunting experiment of this entire training method. Trust the techniques that have already worked for you in previous levels.

Trust that with every minute that passes, energy is following your attention and by directing your intention, it's finding its way into the object.

Be willing to sit at each session for thirty minutes or longer. You must give the energy time to connect with, and accumulate in, the object. Whether or not the object moves, repeat the Stage Three sessions several times per week until you succeed in actualizing the telekinetic effect with significant influence, thus completing your training.

To combat boredom and refresh your confidence, I suggest going back to the Level Two and Level Three exercises once in a while. They will remind you that you are truly capable of performing telekinesis. I mention this because even today when I'm struggling during an advanced level, I find myself wondering if any of it was ever real. People can really be their own worst enemies.

Level Four, Stage Three (Final Stage)

For some real fun, let yourself enjoy the simplicity of Level One. If you haven't been back there in a while, you'll surprise yourself by how much stronger your ability has become since you first started.

Once you feel rested and recharged, continue the Level Four, Stage Three training until you succeed.

Remember, all you have to do is *not give up*.

The feeling of accomplishment of the final stage of Level Four is indescribable. You are now able to have an experience that a great deal of people on this planet believe is utterly impossible. You have gone beyond the generally accepted limits of human ability.

After Level Four, your next question may be, "What's next?"

> To watch videos of Level Four, Stage Three, go to:
> http://www.defyyourlimitsbook.com/eta.html

24. Experiments Beyond Level Four

You've developed the ability to move an object with your mind from a distance. Adding creativity and exploration to your telekinesis practice can keep the topic fun and inspiring. It's also a fantastic way to continually expand your belief system about what's possible in your life.

Here are some ideas for you to try. If they don't interest you, they may at least help you come up with some of your own.

Two people, one object*

Telekinesis can be more fun with a friend. You can try doing Level One, Two, Three, and even Four with someone else. It will become a source of new questions to ponder and explore, such as:

Which one of us is doing it, if not both?

Is either one of us preventing the movement?

How can we work together more successfully?

---

* This and the other experiments in this chapter share a video page on the book's website. The link is at the end of this chapter.

Experiments Beyond Level Four

Using other systems of energy work

Do you practice Tai Chi, Chi Kung, Pranayama or other types of energy work? You could try some exercises that you're already familiar with and combine them with the training method.

Using other types of objects

If you started with tin foil, can you develop your ability with paper? Or cardboard? What if you shaped the tinfoil or paper into a "psi wheel"?* What if you used a much bigger piece of tinfoil? How heavy an object can you move?

Using a scale to measure your strength and grow from there

Keep in mind that if you change to a different object which also seems to weigh very little, it might in fact be many times heavier than what you've been successful with already. For example, when I began experimenting with a beverage can, it felt very light to my hands, and not much heavier than a large piece of tinfoil.

After a long and slow journey with it, I decided to find out what I was really dealing with, and purchased an electronic scale. It turned out that the can weighed over 14 grams. In comparison, an average piece of tinfoil weighed 0.13 grams. The can was *one hundred and seven times* heavier than the tin foil.

---

* An online search for "how to make a psi wheel" will provide you with ample resources.

That's like being able to comfortably lift a 20-pound dumbbell, and then assuming I could lift a 2,000-pound barbell because it *didn't look* that much heavier.

Similar to weight-lifting, I have experienced the gradual strengthening of my own telekinetic influence. Like exercise, my telekinetic effect depends on regular training. If I keep practicing, I slowly increase the weight that I'm able to effect. When I stop, it decreases. Sometimes after a long hiatus, it's like starting all over from the beginning.

You could take the following approach with a scale. Weigh your object, and after becoming skilled with it cut out a bigger piece of tinfoil or paper. Or stack one piece on top of another, gently balancing them on the needle. Test yourself with cutting a can in half, or in quarters,* and seeing if you can move them at all. Track the increasing weight of your objects and see what you learn from doing that.

Larger objects move far easier without the use of a glass container since the flow of energy seems much less obstructed.

Moving two objects under the same container

What happens when you place your intention on two objects at the same time? Will they move simultaneously or

---

* Be careful, the edge of a sliced can is extremely sharp. If you are young, please ask an adult do the cutting for you.

Experiments Beyond Level Four

independently? Is one more responsive than the other? Can you move one, make it stop, then move the other?[*]

Moving an organic object

What if an object has its own life force? Can it respond better than tin foil or paper? Can your energy connect easier to organic substances?

One day, Cierra trimmed a portion of a broad leaf because the tip had deteriorated. Out of curiosity, I balanced the cutting on a needle and found it to be unusually responsive.[**]

Long-Distance Telekinesis

Barbara Lyons is a skilled energy healer in Denver, Colorado. I'd visited her a couple of times for my own healing needs, and mentioned my telekinesis work to her. Because her healing modality is not limited by distance, she suggested a special experiment. She wanted to apply her skills to moving an object from several miles away.

Excited by her proposition, I set up the experiment in my home, which is six miles away from hers. We scheduled a time when the experiment would begin and end.

---

[*] I created this experiment specifically as a response to pseudo-skeptics' claims that convection was the real mechanism behind telekinesis.

[**] I felt alright about using that leaf because it was taken out of care for the whole plant. I personally choose not to take cuttings from healthy plants solely for experimentation. I've learned too much through my own development to do so. The plant has its own energy field. We should wonder then if it has its own awareness. As interconnected beings, I choose not to harm a plant unnecessarily.

I set up my video cameras to record anything that happened during the experiment. The object was tinfoil. The setup was protected by a glass container whose edges were sealed with masking tape to prevent external disturbance.

I stayed in another room during the experiment so that I wouldn't accidentally influence the object. To help keep my attention off the object, Cierra and I enjoyed a nice dinner and talked about other things.

Meanwhile, Barbara spent that period applying her method to the object. The distance was the first challenge. Second, she hadn't even seen the object. She just knew that there was a piece of tin foil in my living room waiting for her to influence it. She was working on the object the same way she treated her long-distance clients: blind.

I watched the video afterward, anxious to see movement, any kind of movement. I became elated after ten minutes when the object finally began a slow and steady swing. Movement and stillness alternated during the remainder of the recorded experiment, at the same time Barbara was *intending it*. I'm certain that it was her influence because there are countless times I've left an object untouched overnight or even longer without it moving at all.

Videos of the above-mentioned demonstrations are here: http://www.defyyourlimitsbook.com/theta.html

Experiments Beyond Level Four

25. Other Objects for Experimentation

A quick search on the internet will show that people are exploring telekinesis with a wide variety of objects. Having learned how to use your attention and intention, you can apply your skill to anything you'd like.

The advantage of the kind of telekinesis you've learned in this training method is that it's an isolatable experiment. The glass container prevents wind movement, and your ability to affect the speed and direction of the object gives evidence that the movement is being directed by your consciousness, not by some ambient physical force.

The disadvantages to the experiments below are that they are far less controlled, which leaves more room for doubt (either by the practitioner or by skeptics and pseudo-skeptics). They may also be far less repeatable which makes learning and development more difficult. Still, it doesn't mean that they're not legitimate. Therefore, you may find it worthwhile to explore these:

Hydrokinesis: The movement of water

An example of this would be to float a small object in a bowl of water and to move it by applying telekinesis to the water molecules that it's floating on.

Electrokinesis: Affecting the flow of electricity

An example would be to cause a light bulb to *flicker*. Focus on interrupting the electrical flow either at the wall outlet or at the base of the bulb where the electricity contacts the filament in a standard bulb.

Another style of electrokinesis is to *illuminate a bulb*. A very small incandescent bulb or an LED bulb is typically used for this. The technique is to generate a flow of energy from one hand to the other, with the bulb in between the hands to close the loop of energy.*

Aerokinesis: The movement of ambient air

Some people practice this outdoors because they can track the wind movement by how it moves nearby trees, bushes, and leaves. Practiced indoors, you could try to influence the air in a room enough to swing a door.

A note about the terms "hydrokinesis," "electrokinesis," and "aerokinesis." These are misnomers because they lack the word "tele." In telekinesis, "tele" refers to the effect across a distance. "Kinesis" means movement. Therefore, telekinesis means movement from a distance, which is what makes it so interesting.

Technically speaking, "hydrokinesis" would only mean *water movement*. It would be more appropriate to call it hydro-

---

* Trebor Seven is an extremely talented telekinesis practitioner and teacher. He has performed this and other types of telekinesis and recorded them. An online search of his name will lead you to his videos.

Other Objects for Experimentation

telekinesis, the movement of water *from a distance*. This way, the psi aspect is reinserted into the term.

Popular terms like "hydrokinesis" will probably retain their common usage though.

26. If You Doubt Your Own Experience

If people's comments make you doubt what you've seen with your own eyes over the last few months of training, remember the following:

You don't need to defend "telekinesis." It's just an idea, nothing can hurt it, and justifying it isn't your job.

You don't have to convince yourself or anyone else that this is telekinesis. If all you can say is that you did something with your mind and body, and the object moved at the same time, and you don't know why, that's alright.

When anyone offers alternative explanations such as heat, static, earthquakes, etcetera, just remember that the object responded specifically to your breathing pattern. If you had the same experiences I did, there were times when you could make the object *stop* on command. Similarly, you could also *reverse it* on command.

If you've been working on this for as long as it took me to reach Level Four, then you've done at least two hundred training sessions. After all that time, you must know with certainty that when you use the techniques, the object responds with a high degree of dependability. Therefore, you know that this isn't random. You're not fooling yourself.

There were probably times during your training when you were steady and really applied yourself, and the object responded sooner and more sensitively to your intention. Then there were other times when you had taken a break, and upon starting again you realized you had sort of "lost it," then had to start over or spend extra time to get back to where you left off.

This "use it or lose it" quality of telekinesis training is another indicator that your consciousness is the driving factor, not ordinary physical effects. Why would heat, static or anything else have a greater effect when you've been practicing a lot, and less of an effect when you haven't been?

We could also ask, if heat, static, or anything else like that did respond to how much you've been training, wouldn't that *still* give evidence for telekinesis and the interaction of consciousness with physical matter?

If someone were to ask you, "Then why hasn't the government approached you about going to work for them?" you can reply that they don't have a need for psychic tinfoil turners. It's easier to just use your hands.

You can also remind them that during the Cold War both Russian and American military and intelligence departments invested money in the development of remote viewing, a type of ESP. On the American side, it was known by its declassified name, Stargate Project.

Today, private organizations and individuals use remote viewing for a variety of objectives ranging from aiding law enforcement in locating missing persons to helping investors profit in the Stock and Commodities markets. The point is that some governments and private organizations *do* take a serious interest in this subject matter.

A final recommendation. Whenever you read or hear someone's opinion about telekinesis, find out who the author is and whether they're a believer, non-believer, skeptic, or pseudo-skeptic. They are each writing their point of view, which they would have you accept as your own.

Be smart, use critical thinking, and always remember that it's just as much about what they won't tell as you as what they will. This applies to online resources like encyclopedias and science pages as well, they were all written by people with personal beliefs.

If You Doubt Your Own Experience

27. An Offering to Science and Spirit

Telekinesis sits at the intersection of science and spirituality. For the scientist, telekinesis is an easily observable phenomenon. Not only can we see it in action, but a practitioner can reproduce the effect. It can be measured, and it can be studied.

In the study of ESP and remote viewing, *giving feedback* means showing the subject the actual target they were trying to perceive from a distance using only their mind.

With ESP, feedback might look like immediately showing the subject the actual playing card whose suit and number they were trying to perceive.

In a remote viewing experiment, feedback is performed by taking the subject to the physical location where their target was located.

In both types of feedback, subjects can quickly discern if their intuition was right or not. This way they can *learn* what they're doing right, and *improve their ability.*

For those learning telekinesis, it offers the advantage of *immediate feedback.* They can see whether or not they are having an effect on the object that very moment. If it moved, they were successful. If it didn't, they weren't.

In terms of spirituality, psi phenomena like telekinesis and ESP are evidence of our interconnectedness. These abilities also promote the idea that who we really are is more than what our eyes can see.

When our body dies, is it possible that some *non-physical* part of us continues on as an integral part of the universe, still capable of perceiving and transmitting information? Does that non-physical aspect give evidence for itself during a telekinesis experiment?

In each telekinesis session, I remind myself that whatever part of me it is which reaches across space, it has no gender, no shape or color, no age, no religion and no nationality. I remember that we all have an aspect of ourselves which is like that. Some call it consciousness, others call it the soul. We can see that our true essence is beyond all those temporary appearances and identifications we use to determine friend and foe.

Telekinesis training is a type of meditation. The basic difference is where the practitioners place their attention. Commonly known meditation techniques instruct practitioners to place their attention on the breath, in the belly, upon a chakra, a mantra, or a visualization. Telekinesis differs simply by having practitioners place their attention on something *out there*.

Because it is something that can be learned through reading books like this or through sheer experimentation, you don't

An Offering to Science and Spirit

need the blessing of an external authority, like a guru or master. You are sacred already, and there's no need for you to surrender your personal power to anyone else.

These are some of the benefits of exploration through telekinesis. We will discuss these spiritual and scientific connections more in the following chapters.

28. Healing, Prayer, Blessing, and ADC

For Energy Healers

Several years after I left my telecommunications career, I decided to become a massage therapist. After a full year of training in a 1,000-hour program, I spent seven years as a full-time therapist in private practice.

Because I was already a meditation practitioner, it was easy for me to relax my mind and body during a session. It was only natural then that over time and with certain clients, I developed an ability to send and receive particular sensations through my hands and with my intention, all for the purpose of healing. This was largely accidental since I didn't advertise myself as an energy worker, only as a physically based massage therapist who employed neuro-muscular therapy.

Much of my clientele was composed of athletes and people who used their bodies a lot at work. They usually came to me with problems caused by overtraining, overuse, and repetitive motion. I also saw clients who wanted to simply relax because they were stressed out or emotionally overwhelmed. Some talked a lot, others were silent, and some would have a good healthy cry.

No matter why they came, one thing was true for all of them: the body and mind affect each other directly. The mind could be used to help the body, and vice versa. After an hour of lying down and just talking to me about their issues, I could physically *feel* the release occurring in their bodies. This is the healing capacity of feeling heard, of *being paid attention to* in an open and non-judgmental manner.

Working the connection in reverse, I could locate a specific point of tension, such as the back of the neck or the lower back, and by massaging that area bring about a *mental and emotional release*. By *paying attention* to where their tension was held in the body, the client became aware of hidden thoughts and emotions. This awareness led to release, which benefitted their whole being.

Both examples above were simply the application of A&I, just like in telekinesis training, but toward another person instead of an object.

I share the following experience for people interested in becoming energy workers in case it's beneficial to them in their healing development.

At one point, I naturally began to feel energy not only in my body, but my clients' bodies. I had gradually become more sensitive to bio-energy through repetition and quiet, open attention. Sometimes the energy felt like heat, sometimes it had a velvety feeling. It could also have a sense of movement, ease and flow to it, or it could feel hard, stuck, or frozen. These words can only approximate what the real experience was like.

I learned to communicate with that other person's energy not only at the point of injury but also with their overall field. Sometimes I would just *listen to it* the way I would listen to the person talk. Other times, when it seemed appropriate, I would *intend it* to soften, flow, let go, or otherwise shift. I instinctually knew to root my intention in the spirit of compassion, openness, and patience.

You probably already know how important it is to set one's ego aside and to not demand results with this type of work. We might not know whether a patient's life path is *meant to include* an illness or not. Sometimes the client could feel the effect, and sometimes they couldn't. An energy worker must remain open to either possibility.

These telekinesis exercises are an excellent way for you to develop your A&I, your attention and intention. By seeing its effect on an external object you'll have far more confidence that your work with the human (or animal) body is real.

Fortunately, your healing energy and your client's energy, regardless of being in a state of health or dis-ease, is all non-physical. Affecting non-physical things like another's energy is far *easier* to do than moving a physical object.

In the chapter *Working with the Eyes*, I explained how to take guidance from the subconscious mind. I use the word "subconscious" here to mean something other than your ordinary thinking, analytical mind. That lesson can also be applied to healing work. It teaches you how to engage in deep listening with your mind. It's a way of gaining information about a patient on the non-physical level.

Healing, Prayer, Blessing, and ADC

I had the opportunity to translate telekinesis into a healing modality several months after my initial success moving an object. I had injured my psoas muscle in a section just below one side of my waist. The pain had been keeping me awake one night, when I decided to experiment with healing myself. Even though it had been years since I had worked as a massage therapist, I was surprised that I hadn't thought of doing this sooner.

I gently pressed the pads of my fingers into the area of pain and simultaneously began *listening* to the muscle tissue. I sent my attention below my fingers into the area where the pain was emanating, and paid close attention to both the physical and energetic sensations there. After some time, I knew that I had *entrained* with that part of my body, that my mind was intimately connected to it.

At that point, I sent my intention into that area for the muscle to relax, for the pain to subside, and for it to receive the rest of the body's natural healing effort. I did this for about a half hour, and once the pain had subsided enough I was able to fall asleep. The next day I awoke in a significantly improved state.

Since then, I've successfully applied those same basic steps above when my wife and others close to me have invited me to experiment with them in times of pain or illness. Their positive reports can only be regarded as anecdotes, of course, so I won't go into detail here. I'll only add that *practicing* this technique serves to improve one's healing ability. For readers who progress all the way to Level Four, this information gives enough guidance for them to do their own experiments with healing.

I hope that healers benefit from this material because although moving a piece of tinfoil or paper from a few feet away doesn't really serve a productive purpose, using the same skills for healing people and animals is extremely worthwhile.

Prayer

I have a childhood memory of accompanying my mom as she did the *Stations of the Cross*. This is a series of prayers done at various stations in a church which mark significant moments in the day when Jesus was crucified. I saw her and others in the group spending long moments with eyes closed in quiet contemplation after reciting a liturgy. This type of prayer was very different from the brisk meal-time prayer we recited at home and *out of habit* more than anything else.

I know that it was a powerful thing for my mom to do because of the way she cried during her contemplation. She was having an experience that I can't pretend to know. Children tend to remember powerful and sometimes awkward moments for the rest of their lives. This was one of those moments for me. When I think about the transformative power of prayer, I remember that day.

When I was in third grade, I had to miss a week of school because of an emergency appendectomy. The day I returned, I was surprised and embarrassed to learn that my mom had visited my classroom while I was in the hospital. She had asked my classmates to pray for me.

How much attention and intention would a room full of third graders be capable of? I don't know, but I trust that it could only have helped. Prayer circles across the world gather regularly to try to positively affect people's lives. Just like a telekinesis practitioner affects an object from a distance, prayer circles do the same for people.

Prayer is simply applying one's A&I in a particular manner. If you're interested in prayer, I suggest telekinesis as a way for you to empower yourself. It can be a tool to regulate your noisy thinking mind and to enhance your quiet, intentional awareness.

All you have to do is use your mind during prayer the same way you do during a telekinesis training session. You'll reach the *potent state* of prayer when your relaxation, breathing, attention and intention are gracefully synchronized.

If you want to make a wireless phone call to God, a deity, spirit, or to the greater unified consciousness of the universe, wouldn't you like the transmission to be as crisp and clear as possible? Telekinesis training can help.

In 2006, Masaru Emoto first published his book, *The Hidden Messages in Water*. Highly acclaimed and immensely popular, his work revealed the effect that our thoughts and feelings could have on water molecules. The effects were obtained by exposing water to words, prayers, and music. Water samples were then frozen, and the resultant crystals photographed.

Uplifting, loving, and inspired words and music caused the water to produce beautiful and harmonious crystals. Hateful and otherwise negative messages produced equally unattractive crystals.

Emoto's work is a beautiful example of how interconnected our world is. It illustrates the power of a blessing - a positive intention directed to someone or something to induce a positive effect. As the majority of the body is composed of water, it's important to consider how our attitudes and opinions can impact it, as well as those of others, directly.

Does the *blessing effect* end with water? I don't think so. People pray or otherwise *use their intention* to bless events, locations, and even the ecosystem. As we know, it is a common practice across cultures to bless one's food before eating.

Just like prayer, the act of blessing can be performed briskly as a symbolic ritual, or it can be done in a way that causes real, beneficial change. In helping you develop the strength of your A&I, telekinesis training can aid your ability to *bless*.

After-Death Communication

Have you ever heard about someone who has died and then sent a loved one *a sign* that they're still around and watching over them? If you've seen the movie *Ghost** with Patrick Swayze or *Dragonfly* with Kevin Costner, then you already have. In *Ghost*, Swayze's character, a disembodied spirit, works at moving physical objects in order to communicate with the living. In *Dragonfly*, Costner's character's wife has passed over, and she sends messages to her husband through the children in the hospital where he works.

Because those are Hollywood movies, a person might assume that these kinds of things don't actually happen. But they do. *The Hand on The Mirror* by Janis Heaphy Dunham is a true account of Dunham's experiences after the death of her husband Max Besler in 2004. It begins with a mysterious hand print on a mirror, and follows with other meaningful, yet strange, signs that could only have been sent by him.

A particularly inspiring true life account of After Death Communication is *Testimony of Light*, by Helen Greaves. Greaves and her close friend Frances Banks spent considerable time learning to communicate telepathically with each other while they were both alive. Sometime after Banks' passing, the communication between them began anew, made possible at least in part by the development they had done together in the physical.

Do you ever think about what it will be like after you die? I certainly do, and accounts like those of Dunham and Greeves

---

* *Dragonfly* (2002). Tom Shadyak. *Ghost* (1990). Jerry Zucker

Healing, Prayer, Blessing, and ADC

inspire me to consider new possibilities. If I were to die before my wife does, I would certainly want to send her a sign somehow. I know that she would do the same for me. Now, after having learned telekinesis, I think I have a way.

My theory is that the deceased have to use their A&I the same way we do while in our bodies. Assuming the involvement of subtle energy, the amount available to a living practitioner is limited because so much energy is required to be inside a body to keep it going. The dead* don't have this problem. Might they have more capacity then, to affect the physical world and *send a sign?***

If so, is telekinesis something they would still need to learn on the other side? If so, I wonder if a spirit might ever wish that he or she had begun their training while on *this* side, the land of the physical.

Would you like to leave a penny or a feather for your child or spouse to discover after you've crossed over? How about subtly directing them to notice an unopened envelope, some words of love that you wanted them to find? Actions like these can help immensely with the grieving process.

What a gift it could be.

---

* I use the word "dead" loosely. I think it's a misnomer since their consciousness is still active. They just happen to exist without physical form.
** These types of signs are called "apports." I highly recommend learning about the *Scole Experiment* for anyone interested in afterlife applications of this material. http://www.thescoleexperiment.com

29. For fans of *The Secret, The Law of Attraction,* and the use of Vision Boards

Do you use a vision board? A vision board is a place to attach picture and phrases that represent your personal goals. Practitioners of *the power of intention* are instructed to look at their board every day and contemplate it. Doing so is said to affect their subconscious awareness and help them achieve their goals. They are also taught that this exercise can invoke changes in the external world to bring them the opportunities necessary to realize their dreams.

I would not be surprised if some people have experienced unquestionable results with their vision board while others haven't. I suspect it has to do with not only how they apply their intention during the exercise, but *how it affects their consciousness.*

In the section *Time Blurring and Sleep Visions,* I shared my early experiences of seeing the object turning in my mind's eye as I went to sleep.

As I mentioned, I suspect that this spontaneous image arose because a change was happening in my consciousness after doing so much training. That change may have been a prerequisite to *manifesting* the idea of telekinesis in physical reality.

How could this information help someone with their vision board? The process is similar to the telekinesis instructions. Let's pretend that your goal is to complete a marathon next year. The photograph on your vision board is of a runner crossing the finish line at the Boston Marathon. How could you combine your telekinesis training with the way you relate to the photograph?

You could begin with a brief telekinesis session, using it as a tool to clarify and relax your mind and to warm up your attention and intention. Once the you've spent a few minutes moving the object, you'll know that you're ready for the next step.

You would then glance at the photograph to shift to the next stage in the process. Before, you wanted to move an object at a distance, and now your goal is to finish a race. You could let the photograph stimulate the feelings of joy, celebration, and achievement you know you'll feel when you cross the finish line. You'll feel the celebration as well as the strength and endurance of that "future you" right now *in this moment*. You can then fold your A&I into the exercise, and direct your subtle energy *into the experience itself.*

The energy will infuse the whole experience and *stimulate your consciousness to change* so that it more resembles that of a successful runner. On the most practical level, doing this before every practice run will keep you inspired enough to overcome the urge to skip or procrastinate.

Running a marathon is similar to telekinesis training in that to reach your goal, all you have to do is *not give up.*

30. Meditation and the Internal Arts

As I shared in the beginning of the book, I've applied the skills I learned from meditation to telekinesis. Many of the meditation techniques I learned employed the directing of one's attention toward specific physical and energetic areas of the body.

Today, the words aura, chakra, chi, dan tien, shushumna, and prana* are almost common parlance among modern spiritual seekers. If you've learned any of those words in the course of your own meditation training, then you've been exposed to one of many different meditative traditions around the world.

The mind and body are intimately connected, and certain types of meditation use both ends of that connection to benefit the other, just like in massage therapy. The state of the subtle energy in the body has a direct impact not only on the physical body, but on the mind, and vice versa.

The difficulty for new meditators is that it can be difficult in the beginning to stabilize one's attention and intention sufficiently to affect one's own subtle energy. Until now, the most common advice given to them has been to "just keep

---

* These words are used in Theosophy, tantric Hinduism and Buddhism, Taoism, and Indian Yoga, among others.

practicing," which I still believe is good advice. Meditation, like any other skill, improves with steady practice and the passage of time.

Telekinesis can serve as a helpful training device for a meditator. In telekinesis, the object's movement serves as a visual feedback device. It only moves when the body and mind are sufficiently relaxed and when one's A&I are tuned in. By training in telekinesis, a meditator can take that experience and transfer it to his or her meditation practice.

For example, let's say your meditation technique involves placing your attention at the chakra on top of your head. If you're having difficulty directing your attention, you can learn the telekinesis exercises. It basically *treats the object like a chakra.*

Instead of drawing your attention and energy someplace in your body, you're pointing them *out there.* Once the visual feedback of the moving object has verified that your mind is steady, you can return to your meditation practice and do the same thing with your body and subtle energy system. You can even use it to explore the ethereal realm of mind, thoughts, and the empty space of awareness from which they appear and disappear.

31. Telekinesis as its own Meditation

In the previous chapter, I described how the telekinesis method can contribute to meditation techniques. Telekinesis can also be experienced as a meditation *in its own right*. Telekinesis offers a unique alternative for those who struggle with other forms of meditation because of boredom or lack of feedback. Once you succeed at telekinesis, it's anything but boring.

Most, if not all forms of meditation share two qualities, *quiescence* and *deliberate placement*. The mind is gradually brought into a state far quieter and subdued than its ordinary mode in daily life. It is brought toward a state of peace.

After entering into quiescence, one's attention can be directed toward an object, such as a mantra, the breath, a prayer, or anything else one likes. Simply put, it's easier to pay attention to something when the mind is at peace. If peace itself is one's goal, then the object of attention serves as a type of anchor for the mind, assisting it in remaining at peace instead of scattering into distraction.

A peaceful mind is a happy mind, though the happiness is different from the ordinary giddiness of buying a new car or eating a slice of cake. This happiness is far more fulfilling because it is born out of a *lack of craving*. Ordinary happiness is limited because when it's created by getting something, as soon as that *thing* is gone, so is the happiness.

Peace from non-craving doesn't have that limitation. It's a state of no longer looking for happiness *out there*, but of feeling complete and whole as a person, from *within*, now.

By now you know that like meditation, telekinesis entails the cultivation of quiescence and deliberate placement. You've learned to not only quiet your mind, but your body as well. The state required for telekinesis is therapeutic that way. Each telekinesis session is a period in your day when you release your stress and cultivate a peaceful state of being.

By repeatedly bringing your attention, intention, and eye-perception to the object, you are strengthening your ability to hold your mind steady. Your trained mind becomes a more effective tool for your consciousness.

If common meditation methods are boring, telekinesis offers the curiosity of a mysteriously moving object. It can be far more interesting than struggling against the boredom of following your own breath.

The movement of the object also acts as a *bio-feedback device* to let you know when you're in a relaxed state.

Every time the object moves, it reminds us that we are not separated from our world, we are not independent. On some level, what we think, say, and do is felt by everyone around us. The reverse is also true. We are the recipients of others' happiness and grief, equally. Telekinesis practice reminds us that we are interconnected, and that knowledge encourages us to be peaceful and kind.

You can't succeed in telekinesis when you're angry or otherwise agitated. The tension in the mind and body is too great. But you can use telekinesis to cool the flames of anger and improve your emotional state.

You can sit down for a regular training session, as upset as you may feel, and start applying the technique. Do a few rounds of the Mind-Stopping-Breath, relax your body, and pay more attention to the object than to whatever it is that's bothering you. If you stick with it long enough, you'll relax, the anger will abate, and your mind will become peaceful.

To convert this telekinesis-type meditation into something truly peaceful, shift from using your intention to move the object to letting go of that action completely. Let go of moving it in any way. As the object comes to stillness, so will your mind. At this level, you shift from *doing* to simply *being*.

If you would like to meditate to quiet the mind, ease away stress and tension, and to tone your mental muscles, this is one way. However, for those who seek the profound transformations* offered by traditional spiritual paths,** you'll need to go beyond telekinesis. It's a great tool for exploration,

---

* A short list of examples: Cessation of suffering (nibbana), non-duality, Christ-consciousness, union with God, the Great Perfection, Higher Self
** ...or your own path. Let's not forget that trail blazing luminaries like Siddhartha Gautama, Jesus of Nazareth and other spiritual founders became who we know them as now because they *departed* from the conventional paths of their time.

Telekinesis as its own Meditation

but the human personality is complex and a complete spiritual journey requires far more than what is offered here.

32. What to Know Before You Show

Potential to Advance Others' Capabilities

You may already know who Roger Bannister is. Until May 6, 1954, most people believed that it was impossible to run a mile in under four minutes. Bannister believed that he could, and on that date, he ran a mile in three minutes, fifty-nine and fourth tenths of a second.

What is more amazing than this new speed record is that only two months later when Bannister raced against John Landy, *both* of them broke it, surpassing the four-minute mile. Soon after that, more and more people joined the sub-4 club. Once everyone had evidence that it could be done, they *believed that they could do it too*, and they did.

Every time I have shown family members or friends what I could do in person, they were able to reproduce the effect themselves within the hour, and often much quicker than that. In these instances, I was using Level Two for its speed of effect. Doing Level Three and Four with an audience takes far too long to keep them interested.

Whereas it had taken me several weeks to succeed with Level Two, it only took *eye witnesses* less than an hour.

I believe this is largely due to the Bannister Effect. If I had only *told* them that I could move an object from a distance, they probably wouldn't believe me. They might believe *that I believed* I was using telekinesis, and probably feel sorry for me. "Why can't he see that he's fooling himself?" they'd ask.

In person, though, they could not only verify the movement, but also observe the setup, the environment, and what I was doing. They would try it themselves, and because they now believed it was really possible, they'd succeed.

Cierra was the first person I showed this to. She succeeded on her first attempt*, which I must admit frustrated the heck out of me because I had worked for so long to do what she was instantly capable of. I was also excited for her of course, and intrigued about what this could mean for other people.

---

* Those readers who have had dreams in which they performed telekinesis would be interested to know that Cierra had had several lucid dreams before this, in which she moved objects in her dream environment with her intention. We suspect it may have assisted her when the time came to try in waking reality.

Defy Your Limits   Sean McNamara

Choosing Whom to Share This With

I don't think Cierra succeeded merely because she witnessed me doing it. As my loving wife, she believed in me, trusted me, and supported my exploration with her sense of humor and encouragement. These are the same traits shared by the friends and family I've shown this to in person. They trusted me, they were open to the possibility of telekinesis, and they genuinely wanted to see if they could replicate the effect.

People can be fickle though.

After Cierra's success, we decided to demonstrate it for two friends, a married couple. Not only did they watch me do it, they watched Cierra do it too. Then they tried.

The wife succeeded that same evening, but the husband did not. A few days later I asked them if they tried the experiment again on their own, and they responded that they had, but that it didn't work. Also, they ultimately concluded that wind or some other factor had been involved the first time they tried it with us.

Even after our demonstration, they remained unconvinced that telekinesis is real. We could say that their *inner skeptics* and their *inner believers* had been overcome by their *inner non-believers*. Once they decided it wasn't real, there was no reason for them to put the time and effort in to keep trying on their own, and possibly changing their point of view.

If I were to show a person telekinesis, specifically someone who didn't share my first successful friends' positive traits, I'm certain they wouldn't believe their own eyes.

What to Know Before You Show

It is well known that even intelligent scientists upon obtaining data which contradict their personal belief system will either ignore that data, argue that there is a flaw in the experiment, or accuse the experimenter of fraud.

This phenomenon is also known to behavioral economists, people who study human behavior. They study our decision making, preferences, and buying habits. When they assume that humans are rational, logical, and intelligent, the data shows that our behavior indicates otherwise. People are not rational creatures.

We prove over and over to be instinctual and emotional beings whose decisions are influenced by group behavior and environmental cues as much, if not more than, our individual minds.

If you show telekinesis to someone who doesn't believe in it, whose family attitude toward the "paranormal" is negatively biased,* or who would love to have a reason to ridicule you, you'll realize very quickly that you've made a grave mistake.

Yes, that person will walk away with new thoughts in mind, but none of them will be positive toward you or toward what they just witnessed.

---

* Assuming that you have successfully engaged the training method through Level Four, you know now that telekinesis is *not* para-normal, it's *very* normal. We just need more time and resources to understand the mechanism behind it, to learn how it *really* works. Doing so will help to normalize it for general acceptance in society.

But if you teach it to the right person, someone who truly wants to learn it, it can be one of the most transformative gifts you'll ever give someone.

Personal Ethics and Demonstrating Telekinesis

People have an instinctual need for physical security, such as knowing they'll be fed, clothed, and housed. Threatening their access to those things is an assault on their security. They also have a need for *existential security.*

They need to feel secure in their place in the world, in how the world works, and what the rules of participation in life are. Politics and religion usually try to establish those rules for people, although each person ultimately makes his or her own choice about what to believe.

Therefore, we need to be aware that the vast majority of people are quite satisfied with their current belief system. They are also psychologically unprepared for evidence that contradicts what they believe to be true. It can be a profound shock to a person when they discover that things are not what they seem. This is especially true when a person has not sought out that new information through their own volition.

If you introduce the idea of telekinesis to someone, or show it to them, and if you do so without their request, you risk posing a *psychological threat* to that person. Granted, children are fairly open minded and psychologically flexible. The threat really lies with adults who have been firmly programmed by television, religion, community, politics, and their parents' values.

For your sake and theirs, please be careful when deciding whether or not to pull out your tinfoil after dinner and ask if they want to see something cool.

The Difficulty in Video Recording and Showing Others

Almost every time I pressed the *record* button on my video cameras, my telekinesis ability would fade significantly. With the most difficult experiments, it would sometimes fail entirely. The cause for this was obvious to me, it was my self-consciousness. Performance anxiety and concern about public opinion naturally arose within my conscious mind every time I turned the cameras on.

I've seen the footage of the 1973 episode of *The Tonight Show* starring Johnny Carson featuring Uri Geller*. He is world-renowned for psychic abilities such as spoon bending, remote viewing, and dowsing. His spoon-bending influence even extended into the homes of his television viewers. Silverware inside kitchens hundreds of miles away spontaneously bent during his performances.

On this episode of *The Tonight Show*, Geller hadn't been expecting to perform his feats on stage. He seemed shocked and disappointed to see a tableful of experiments waiting before him as he sat down next to his host. Even though he explained to Carson and to the audience that he needed to be in the *right frame of mind*, Carson pressured him to perform. It was plain to see that he wasn't comfortable or in the right state. He seemed uneasy for some reason.

Not surprisingly, he failed to impress Carson and many viewers across America.

---

* Multiple video sources available by searching "Uri Geller on the Tonight Show" online.

What to Know Before You Show

The memory of what happened to Geller only adds to the hesitation and tension that arises whenever I turn on a video camera. It also affects me when showing it to others in person. It takes me longer to move the object, and the movement is less pronounced.

I mention this for anyone who might consider sharing their telekinesis experience with others, either in a live performance or through making videos. If performance anxiety is an issue for you, you'll simply need to learn to relax with it, ideally in private before testing yourself in public. After you've made several videos and become comfortable with the process, it will be much less of an issue.

Personal Risks

I am happy to say that after one hundred thousand views of my online videos I've only been accused of witchcraft a handful of times. This is a welcomed indication that society is progressing.

Many people are familiar with the Salem witch-trials, which were nothing more than an event of mass hysteria used to kill innocent people, which occurred in the 17th century. Yet we should also remember that in 1944, Helen Duncan became the last person to be convicted in Britain for violation of the Witchcraft Act of 1735. That was *less than a century ago.*

Today, forward-thinking scientists have to take great care in what kind of phenomena they research, and who they share their findings with. They know too well that they risk their credentials, their teaching appointments, their funding, and their reputation for advancing psi research.

Simply put, be cautious when deciding whether or not to let your social circle know that you can move things with your mind.

33. Skeptics and Pseudo-Skeptics

Internet trolls, non-believers, and pseudo-skeptics have one thing in common: they are not interested in changing their belief system. They firmly believe telekinesis isn't real. And they will always be right in their own mind. Even if you had the opportunity to sit with them, show it to them, and teach them how to do it themselves, they probably wouldn't do it.

However, true skeptics, which some, but not all, scientists are, deserve respect. You can identify them by the nature of their communication. They'll say things like:

I'm not sure about what I'm seeing here. But I remain undecided, and I'm willing to wait.

Can you help me understand what it is I'm seeing here?

I'd like to try to do this myself. Can you give me the necessary information to do so?

Can you recommend any published scientific findings from reputable sources?

When responding to skeptics, the onus is on you to be honest, fair, and helpful. It's not to convince them that you're right. Anyway, they wouldn't let you because they want to find out for themselves, just as *you* did when you opened the first page of this book. So, help them out.

Can you explain your technique in a clear and understandable manner? Can you refer them to published scientists and researchers, or to other practitioners? Skeptics are our friends because we can share in peaceful and honest inquiry with them. They help us all to learn more.

Finally, don't be afraid to acknowledge what you don't know, or don't understand, and what you can and cannot do. True skeptics will respect you for your honesty. It shows that you're not trying to convert them, but that you are as interested in exploring what's real as much as they are.

Skeptics and Pseudo-Skeptics

34. It's Only a Matter of Time...

It's not telekinesis, it's science! Typical online commenters continue by describing their explanations for what they see. Here are some examples from my own viewers:

It's static.

It's subterranean tremors, vibrating up into the house and moving it. Happens all the time.

It's your hands heating the glass and causing the air to circulate, which moves it.

It's the sunlight hitting the reflective surface, which pushes it.

It's not telekinesis, it's physics.

That last one makes me smile. Because *I think they're right.*

When they use the word "telekinesis" in that statement, I think they believe *that I believe* that telekinesis is some kind of magic - some unexplainable, illogical, and imaginary force, like a superstition. And when they refer to "physics" they're implying that there has to be a real cause for the movement.

I think that there *is* a measurable cause for the movement, one that is a natural part of our world. We just don't know *how* to measure it yet.

I have referred to most of my ideas as mental models and working hypotheses from the very beginning of this book. I recognize that although these ideas are what made it possible for me to have an effect with a physical object distant from me in space, I can't say that they accurately represent what's really happening.

It's only a matter of time before we can measure whatever it is that's involved. I'm sure it's something that has always existed, just like electromagnetic forces.

Telekinesis may even *be* an electromagnetic force. If it is, then what makes telekinesis special is the fact that a human being *can direct this force* by his or her attention, intention, and will – by *the mind*.

Here's one of my favorites, *It's not telekinesis, it's chi.*

As in the earlier objection, this pseudo-skeptic asserts that the effect is produced by an alternative mechanism. In this case, however, he or she proposes *chi* as the alternative, something which until recently would have been considered just as unreal as telekinesis. I regard comments like this as signs of society's progress.

35. Becoming More Contemplative

Today's culture generally does not value contemplative activity or time spent in silence. Instead, it promotes consumerism, the pursuit of happiness through watching entertainment on television and the internet, and by buying stuff. In contrast to past societies or today's rare indigenous cultures whose spiritual roots have been preserved, modern society is bereft of silent contemplation.

All of us who strive to make prayer, meditation, and even exercise a part of daily life face one significant struggle: we've been programmed by our environment* to spend our non-working hours in front of an electronic screen and to be entertained.

How many personal dreams and inspirations have remained in the realm of thought instead of being manifested because a person had a daily habit of being entertained instead?

We've been programmed into maintaining a state of complacency. Instead of making our mark in life, we tend to

---

* *Environment* is defined here as the habitual behavior of one's friends, family, and overall culture, as well as the objects which are placed in focus-areas of one's home. Until the invention of the radio, then of the television, an altar, shrine, or other place designated for contemplation would have taken the primary position in one's home.

Defy Your Limits   Sean McNamara

sit on the couch and watch what others have accomplished. Every few minutes a commercial comes on and, through simple repetition, shapes our ideas about life and happiness so that we spend money they way an advertiser wants us to.

Looking at this through the lens of telekinesis, we could say that when we watch TV and the internet *we open our mind indiscriminately and expose it to someone else's intentions.* We become *the object* of someone else's experiment.

Whether you want to succeed at telekinesis, meditation, writing that novel you've always had inside of you, playing the piano, or creating a business plan so you can leave your dead-end job, it's likely that your biggest enemy is right there in your living room. Avoid it as much as you can.

36. Universal Principles for Success in Life

Those of you who have trained successfully all the way through Level Four know that your success wasn't because you possessed some mysterious quality. You succeeded for the same reason so many other trail blazers, entrepreneurs, inventors, business people, leaders and artists have reached their goals, and in many cases changed the world.

During the many weeks and months that you've been training in telekinesis, you've been applying life's *universal principles for success*, which you can apply to other areas of your life. I will list them here in simple form to refresh your memory.

The Universal Principles

You were *motivated*. You had a personal reason to see this through, all the way.

You were *passionate* about it. You were excited, inspired, and driven to do this.

You were *self-driven*, you showed *persistence*. It was just you and this book. You kept going even when you felt like giving up. You did it for *you* and no one else.

You had *integrity*. You weren't willing to call it a success until you were sure of what you were seeing and had eliminated any possible outside causes. You weren't interested in illusions, only the real thing.

You were able to *not worry what other people might think* if they knew you were doing this. If any non-believers or pseudo-skeptics came on the scene, you didn't waste energy trying to change their belief systems. You knew that only they could change their own minds.

You *listened to your inner-believer and inner-skeptic*. The believer in you kept you going, gave you faith in yourself. The skeptic in you helped you learn what science has discovered so you could let go of outdated beliefs that would hold you back. *You did the research* necessary to stay informed.*

You *trained regularly*, even daily. You knew that progress only came with practice. You knew that the surest way to fall short was to stop training before reaching your goal.

You never said "It's not working!" You *didn't blame* someone or something else. You did whatever troubleshooting was necessary. You got creative with the technique, and you found your way.

---

* About doing research and reading. In my line of work, I visit a lot of people's homes. One thing I notice is that those of wealthy people usually have offices or libraries filled with books. These books typically focus on self-development, financial management, personal or spiritual values, and education. In the homes of low or middle income families, the bookshelves are usually stocked with DVD's and books which I'd qualify as entertainment-focused. A message to the reader, especially if you are a young person – you become what you put in your mind.

Universal Principles for Success in Life

You knew that every session was important, whether or not the object moved. You didn't measure or compare your results every five or ten minutes. You put all your effort into the exercise, only *waiting until you saw the result* before measuring yourself.

You *stayed true* to the instructions. Instead of giving up in the middle of a session and desperately trying out a completely different method, you *remained steady with the technique*. You gave it the necessary time to produce results.

You applied the working hypothesis that *energy follows attention*. That principle didn't just apply to telekinesis, it applied to the whole training. *You kept your attention on the goal* of reaching Level Four, not just one of the lower levels. Your focus on the final goal filled your life with the energy that would take you there.

You learned to *stay relaxed* and undistracted at the same time.

You dared to *try the impossible*. You also learned to gain information from beyond the five physical senses.

You learned to *follow your intuition*, to take guidance from the impulses emerging out of your subconscious.

You *entrained* with the object. You *developed a relationship with it* instead of regarding it as something completely separate from you. You were engaged with *the other*.

You *didn't skip* any steps. You recognized that you have to start with a strong foundation before building the rest of the house.

When you succeeded at Level One, you moved on to Level Two, and so on. You constantly learned more and *transcended your comfort zone.*

When you needed to rest, you did. You were careful not to burn yourself out. *You looked after yourself.*

Telekinesis may seem difficult, but there are far more difficult goals in life. What do you want to achieve in life? Who would you like to become? How do you want to benefit this world?

Whatever you decide to do, I hope these principles assist you along the way.

37. We Are One

The knowledge that our perceived separateness from each other and from our world is *merely an illusion* has existed in human consciousness for thousands of years, passed on through ancient spiritual tradition. Today, this idea still finds its voice in the Indian Yoga tradition, particular philosophies of Buddhism, and teachings on Non-Duality, among others.

Philosophers and scientists are adopting concepts from quantum physics and finding parallels with these spiritual perspectives. Though I'm not scientifically qualified to speak about these ideas,* I will share observations from my own telekinesis experience. For me, personal observation always supersedes theories, no matter how spectacular the theories seem.

Do you recall the anomaly I mentioned earlier? I described how once in a while, the object would begin turning just as I entered the room. I had entered and exited the training area hundreds of times, so if the movement was just the result of my footsteps, it would have become obvious. Also, the object didn't react that way when other people, people who weren't

---

* I also dislike the popular use of quantum theory in *some* self-help publications because of the difficulty in proving the successful application of their ideas. This is the advantage of telekinesis, that you can see it immediately with your own two eyes.

entrained with the object, also entered into the room. It had a *relationship with me.*

That idea is enough for me to consider that these ancient teachings and modern hypotheses might be accurate. Although I'd only actualized my connection with specific objects during my telekinesis training, it doesn't mean that an inherent connection doesn't already exist between us and everything else in this world.

Another occurrence is related to this experience. Most of the time, the object "behaved" and kept still as I entered the room and sat down in front of it. Yet before I had consciously begun the experiment and directed my attention to it, it would begin to turn. I wouldn't go so far as to say it was reading my mind. Rather, I'm more inclined to wonder if it was skipping ahead in time, into the future.

Research and theoretical explorations in quantum physics describe subatomic particles being capable of appearing in two places at the same time, and also disappearing and reappearing into past and future moments,[*] albeit very, very quickly.

There have been instances when I would work with an object for a while, finding no success, no movement at all. I would stand up to take a break. Sometimes I'd stay right there, other times I'd walk a few steps away, or exit the room. Spontaneously, the object would move, significantly. The movement was bigger and faster than usual.

---

[*] See Zukav, Gary (1979), *The Dancing Wu Li Masters*

Earlier in this book I hypothesized that energy accumulates in an object over time, and that a certain amount is required for motion to occur. I also mentioned that sometimes in the moment of giving up my efforts, the object would only then begin to move. This indicated that something in my mind had been preventing the movement.

Odd as it may sound, when this occurs, it feels like the object is actually catching up in time. I use the word "feels" because this is more of an intuition than an observation for me.

There's a reason why I bring up the question of time. During some of my early experiments I'd sit with the object and, while keeping the physical image in mind I'd simultaneously visualize its next moment. This next moment was a version of reality in which the object had begun to move. During Level Two, I called this *time blurring*.

After picturing the object in motion, the future version of the one before me, I'd mentally pull that image into the present, overlaying it upon the image of the still object. I was trying to intend a future potential moment into entering the present one. What if that method was actually effective?

We might not only be *unified in space*, mutually connected at all points, but we might also be *unified in time*. The separateness of future, present and past might be as illusory as the separateness between you, me, and the things of this world.

Telekinesis can serve as a reminder that all people share the same essence. Whatever that part of me is which extends beyond the skin boundary of my body, it has no color, no gender, no religion, or any of the other surface level distinctions we use to sort each other out. Every person's consciousness surpasses these distinctions. It is our ineffable nature which unites us.

I hope that your experience with telekinesis encourages your sense of empathy, compassion, and unity with all people.

We're all doing the best we can.

We Are One

Epilogue

As practitioners of psi phenomena, particularly telekinesis, we have important contributions to make in the realms of science, spirituality, and society.

Scientific researchers need subjects for their experimental trials. Their data can only reflect the abilities of those people who step forward to work with them. I imagine that researchers gain far more from working with talented subjects than with those who have never exercised their latent capacities. I imagine there are scientists out there who would benefit from meeting someone like you.

As science progresses, it comes closer to backing up some of the most ancient and beneficial tenets of spirituality. The data are reflecting some of our beliefs, that we are interconnected (if not completely unified), that our thoughts and actions affect others, and that if we have faith in our abilities then we can ascend to new heights of experience. In this way, psi research serves as a place where science and spirituality can meet and exchange ideas.

Further research will help to reduce society's general fear and ignorance of psi phenomena. This will allow more people just like you to freely learn how to do things which used to be regarded as negative or dangerous. I imagine a day when parents "play telekinesis" with their children as a way of showing them their non-physical aspect. Readers like you could start "telekinesis clubs" and practice in groups. Perhaps the Bannister effect will take effect and help to accelerate public knowledge of these inherent abilities.

What you do with your ability is up to you. It could be something you dip your toes into and then, curiosity satiated, you move on. Or you could make it your own personal meditation, your way of relaxing mind and body on a daily basis. It could be your bio-feedback device. Many other doors are open to you now.

After all the reminders to not stray from the instructions, it's time for me to suggest you let them go. If you've succeeded through Level Four, you don't need them anymore. If you rely on them for future explorations, they might hold you back. It's time for you to clear a new path, to develop new techniques that will help all of us evolve further.

Are you a teacher at heart? Offering it to those who want to learn about it could be a valuable thing to do, for you and your future students. Telekinesis should never become the restricted property of a person, tradition, or community.

It's inside all of us.

Epilogue

The Web Site, Video and Audio, Practitioner Survey, and the Question & Answer Section

Introduction to the Site, Finding the Page Links

A special web page has been created to assist your development, http://www.DefyYourLimitsBook.com

This site contains videos that are new to the public, and which were created specifically for readers of this book.

The links to the specific pages are written in their respective chapters. The home page for the site does not contain a page menu in order to maintain privacy, since the videos are only understandable by those who have the book and who are engaging the training system presented here.

Online Survey for Telekinesis Practitioners

The web site also has a survey for practitioners. I hope you'll be interested in filling it out. Once significant data

is obtained it will be posted to the site.

Defy Your Limits   Sean McNamara

> You can find the survey at:
> http://www.defyyourlimitsbook.com/kappa.html

Question & Answer Section

If you want to ask me a question, a Question and Answer Page is available. The answers will be posted in order to help other practitioners in their development.

> You can find the Q&A page here:
> http://www.defyyourlimitsbook.com/lambda.html

References

Cherylee Black - My NDEs, aftereffects and what I'm doing about them now. (2015, July 23). Retrieved from https://www.youtube.com/watch?v=MZpBV3BZ1lc

Emoto, Masaru (2005). The Hidden Messages in Water. Atria Books.

Greaves, Helen (2009). Testimony of Light, An Extraordinary Message of Life After Death. (first American edition) London: Penguin Books Ltd.

Hicks, E. & Hicks, J. (2006). The Law of Attraction, The Basics of the Teachings of Abraham. Hay House.

Olds, Robert and Rachel. (2014). Primordial Grace, Earth, Original Heart, and the Visionary Path of Radiance. Heart Seed Press.

Radin, Dean (2013). Supernormal, Science, yoga, and the Evidence for Extraordinary Psychic Abilities. New York: Random House, Inc.

The Secret. (2006). [DVD] Rhonda Byrne & Paul Harrington.

Tart, Charles T. (2009). The End of Materialism, How Evidence of the Paranormal is Bringing Science and Spirit Together. Oakland: New Harbinger Publications, Inc.

Recommended Resources

Books

Buhlman, William. (1996). Adventures Beyond the Body, How to Experience Out-of-Body Travel. New York: HarperCollins Publishers.

Champlain, Sandra (2013). We Don't Die, A skeptic's Discovery of Life After Death. Morgan James Publishing.

Devananda, Swami Vishnu (1988). The Complete Illustrated Book of Yoga. New York: Three Rivers Press.

Gallenberger, Joe. (2013). Inner Vegas: Creating Miracles, Abundance, and Health. Rainbow Ridge Books.

Guggenheim, G. & Guggenheim, J. (1995) Hello from Heaven! A new field of research ~After-Death Communication~ confirms that life and love are eternal. New York: Random House.

Laszlo, E. & Peake, A. (2014) The Immortal Mind, Science and the Continuity of Consciousness Beyond the Brain. Rochester: Inner Traditions.

Liao, Waysun. (1990). T'ai Chi Classics. Boston: Shambhala Publications, Inc.

222

Lipton, Bruce H. (2008). The Biology of Belief, Unleashing the Power of Consciousness, Matter & Miracles. Hay House, Inc.

McMoneagle, Joseph. (2000). Remote Viewing Secrets, A Handbook. Charlottesville: Hampton Roads Publishing Company, Inc.

Olson, Stuart Alve. (2002). Qigong Teaching of a Taoist Immortal, The Eight Essential Exercises of Master Li Ching-Yun. Rochester: Inner Traditions International.

Radin, Dean (2006). Entangled Minds, Extrasensory Experiences in a Quantum Reality. New York: Simon & Schuster, Inc.

Schmidt, Amy (2005). Dipa Ma, The Life and Legacy of a Buddhist Master. New York: United Tribes Media, Inc.

Sinclair, Upton (2001). Mental Radio, Studies in Consciousness (Russell Targ Editions edition). Charlottesville: Hampton Roads Publishing.

Targ, Russell (2004). Limitless Mind, a Guide to Remote Viewing and Transformation of Consciousness. Novato: New World Library.

Yu, Lu K'uan (1973). Taoist Yoga, Alchemy and Immortality. San Francisco: RedWheel/Weiser LLC.

Zukav, Gary (1979), The Dancing Wu Li Masters, An Overview of the New Physics. New York: William Morrow and Company, Inc.

Videos

The Afterlife Investigations. (2011). [DVD]. Tim Coleman.

The Living Matrix. (2007). [DVD}. Greg Becker.

The PEAR Proposition, A Quarter Century of Princeton Engineering Anomalies Research. (2006). [DVD] StripMindMedia.

Solar Revolution. (2003). [DVD]. Dieter Broers.

Public Online Videos*

Eric Pearl - Biology of transformation - The Field. (2012, September 19). Retrieved from https://www.youtube.com/watch?v=_VFxKiwKvYA

Gregg Braden – Cancer cured in 3 Minutes. (2013, September 2). Retrieved from https://www.youtube.com/watch?v=VLPahLakP_Q

Lynne McTaggart - Biology of Transformation - The Field. (2012, September 19). Retrieved from https://www.youtube.com/watch?v=Mtd00qLYPL8

---

* These web links were valid as of the date this book was first published. If the links no longer work, it is recommended that the reader do an internet search using the video title.

Personal Health Summit 2015 #15: Paranormal Science & World Health, with Dean Radin & Matt Riemann. (2015, October 16). Retrieved from https://www.youtube.com/watch?v=xSQBDoEizns

Scientific and Spiritual Implications of Psychic Abilities - Russell Targ. (2015, February 17). Retrieved from https://www.youtube.com/watch?v=zgyYms376Mg

Index

Index

Index

We are capable of so much more than we believe.
Overcome your self-doubt, set your intention, hold steady.
Reality will reveal itself to those who
Dare to look.

- S.M.

Made in the USA
Middletown, DE
20 March 2021